ATLAS OF
CENTRAL & SUBURBAN PLANS
LONDON

Published by the Automobile Association
Fanum House, Basingstoke, Hants RG21 2EA

Route Planning Map

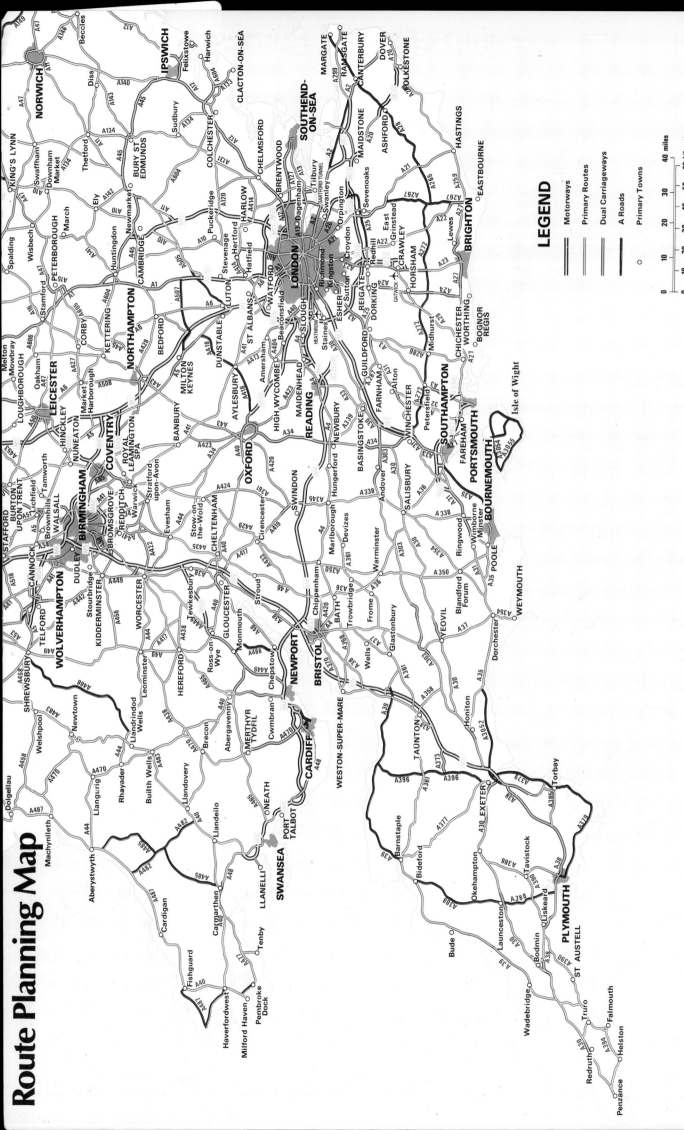

LEGEND

≡≡	Motorways
━━	Primary Routes
━━	Dual Carriageways
━━	A Roads
○	Primary Towns

0 10 20 30 40 miles

0 10 20 30 40 50 60 kilometres

London's Orbital Routes

When the M25 is complete it will form a circular motorway route round London, apart from the section between junctions 2 and 31, linked by the Dartford Tunnel. This map shows the latest available information on the progress of the orbital route. The map also shows the North and South Circular roads and the Inner Ring Road.

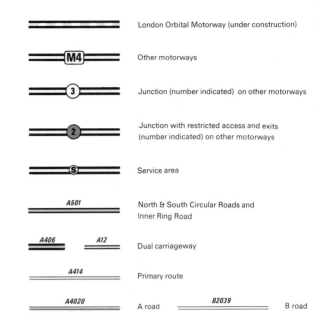

London Orbital Motorway (under construction)

M4 Other motorways

③ Junction (number indicated) on other motorways

② Junction with restricted access and exits (number indicated) on other motorways

Ⓢ Service area

A501 North & South Circular Roads and Inner Ring Road

A406 *A12* Dual carriageway

A414 Primary route

A4020 A road   *B2039* B road

LEGEND

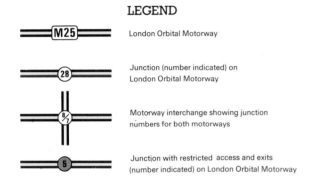

M25 London Orbital Motorway

㉘ Junction (number indicated) on London Orbital Motorway

⑧/⑦ Motorway interchange showing junction numbers for both motorways

⑤ Junction with restricted access and exits (number indicated) on London Orbital Motorway

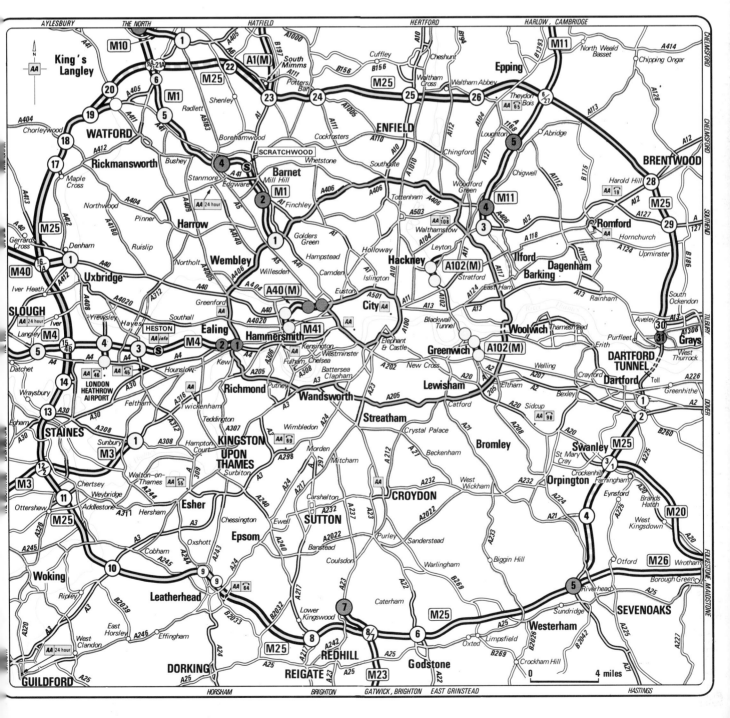

London influences a vast area, and its visible tentacles of buildings and roads stretch far and wide, but many of the towns within its orbit retain a determinedly individual personality. Towns closer to the heart of the capital were little more than hamlets a century ago; often their original cores are preserved almost intact. Some, like Wimbledon and Twickenham, have achieved fame through activities quite unconnected with the world of commerce and industry. London itself has as many facets as a diamond – and like a jewel it exerts a compelling and often mysterious fascination.

There are 68 town plans in this book. Central London is included, of course, but the area covered stretches from Uxbridge in the west to Upminster in the east, and from Enfield in the north to Coulsdon in the south. Area plans and descriptions of the towns are included, and street indexes make the plans practical and easy to use. Heathrow has its own plan and area map.

Produced by the Cartographic Department
Publishing Division of the Automobile Association

The contents of this book are believed correct at the time of printing. Nevertheless, the publisher can accept no responsibility for errors or omissions, or for changes in the details given.

© The Automobile Association 1986

Published by the Automobile Association, Fanum House, Basingstoke, Hampshire RG21 2EA

Printed and bound in Spain by Graficromo SA, Spain

ISBN 0 86145 367 0

AA Ref 57707

London

AREA MAPS ARE INDICATED IN BOLD.

MAP REF	PAGE No	MAP REF	PAGE No	MAP REF	PAGE No
1 Central London	**8-9**	25 Hackney/Dalston	18	48 Purley	13
2 Theatreland	**11**	26 Hammersmith	14	49 Putney	45
3 Barking	**2**	27 Hampstead	23	**50 Richmond**	**34**
4 Barkingside	24	28 Harlesden	46	**51 Romford**	**36**
5 Barnet	**4**	**29 Harrow**	**20**	52 Southall	14
6 Battersea	45	30 Hayes	40	53 Stanmore	20
7 Beckenham	7	**31 Heathrow Airport**	**48**	54 Stoke Newington	18
8 Bermondsey	30	**32 Hendon**	**22**	55 Stratford	2
9 Brentford	35	33 Holloway	26	56 Streatham	30
10 Brixton	31	34 Hornchurch	37	57 Surbiton	29
11 Bromley	**6**	35 Hounslow	35	**58 Sutton**	**38**
12 Carshalton	39	**36 Ilford**	**25**	59 Tottenham	26
13 Coulsdon	12	**37 Islington**	**26**	60 Twickenham	34
14 Croydon	**12**	**38 Kingston**	**28**	61 Upminster	37
15 Dalston	18	**39 Lambeth/**		**62 Uxbridge**	**40**
16 Ealing	**14**	**Bermondsey**	**30**	**63 Walthamstow**	**42**
17 East Ham	2	**40 Lewisham**	**32**	**64 Wandsworth**	**44**
18 Edgware	4	41 Leyton	43	**65 Wembley**	**46**
19 Edmonton	17	42 Leytonstone	43	66 West Drayton	40
20 Eltham	32	43 Loughton	24	67 Willesden	47
21 Enfield	**16**	44 Mitcham	39	68 Wimbledon	38
22 Epsom	29	45 Orpington	7	**69 Wood Green**	26
23 Finchley	4	46 Palmers Green	17	70 Woolwich	32
24 Greenwich	32	47 Peckham	30	71 Yiewsley	40

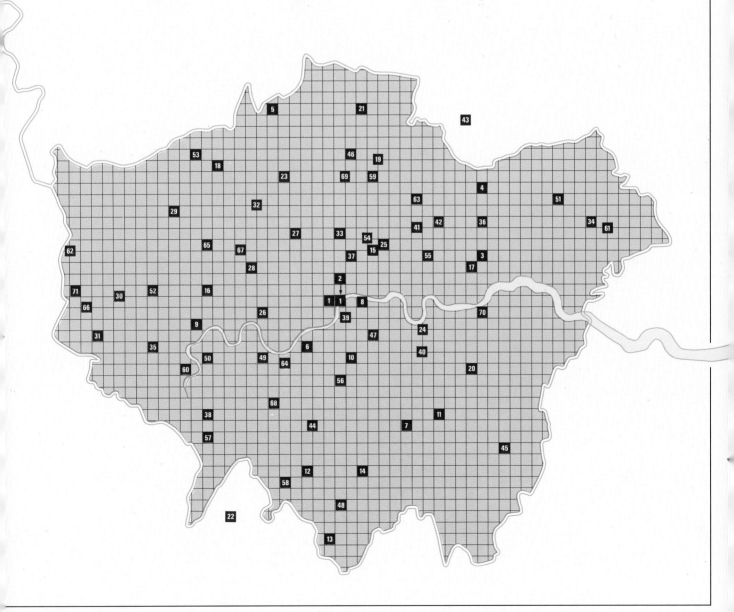

Barking

A flourishing fishing industry operating from the Town Quay was the mainstay of Barking until well into the 19th century, when the coming of the railways and easy access to the east coast ports brought about its decline. The area has since undergone a good deal of industrial development but Barking still has a number of pleasant parks, notably Barking Park, which has a miniature railway and a large open air swimming pool. Still to be seen are the remains of Barking Abbey (founded in the 7th century and focus of the original settlement), Eastbury House, which dates from the 16th century, and the 13th-century Parish Church of St Margaret, where Captain Cook, the explorer, was married in 1762.

East Ham's Central Park is the scene of the colourful Town Show staged by the Borough of Newham each year. Dating back to Roman times, this ancient parish saw heavy development during the late 19th century, when most of the local industry was centred around the nearby docks.

Stratford Controversial new productions are the speciality of the Victorian Theatre Royal, a local landmark near the modern shopping centre. Site of a Roman fording of the River Lea, Stratford also has the Passmore Edwards Museum, which was built to house the collections of the Essex Field Club and now deals with local history and archaeology.

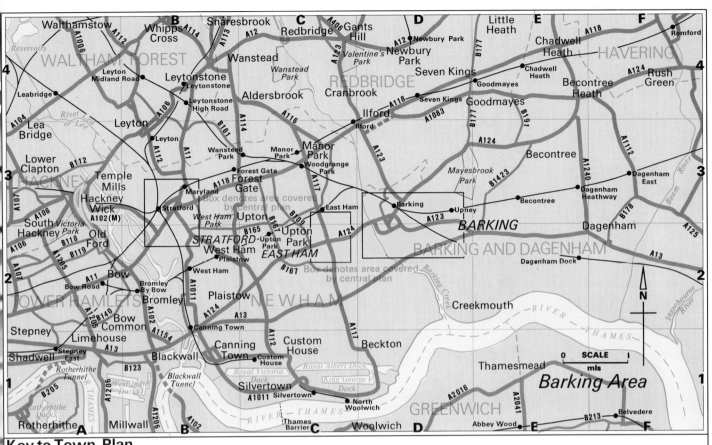

Key to Town Plan and Area Plan

Town Plan
AA Recommended roads
Other roads
Restricted roads
Buildings of interest School
Churches †
Car Parks P
Parks and open spaces
BR and Underground Stations ⊖
One way streets ←

Area Plan
A roads
B roads
Stations Woodside
Borough boundary

Street Index with Grid Reference

Barking

Abbey Road	A3-A2-B2-B1
Aldersey Gardens	C4-D4
Alfreds Gardens	D1-E1
Bamford Road	B4
Barking By-Pass	D1-E1-F1-F2
Beccles Drive	E4
Blake Avenue	E2-F2
Boundary Road	B1-C1
Broadway	B2
Buller Road	D3-D4
Cecil Avenue	C3-C4
Charlton Crescent	E1-F1
Church Road	B4
Clare Gardens	F4
Cowbridge Lane	A3-B3
Cranbourne Road	C2-D2
Cranleigh Gardens	C4
Dawson Avenue	E3-F3
Denham Way	E2
Devon Road	D2-E2
Digby Road	E3
Eastbury Square	
East Street	B2-B3-C3
Edgefield Avenue	F3-F4
Eldred Road	D2
Essex Road	C3-D3-D2
Faircross Avenue	B4-C4
Fanshawe Avenue	B4-C4
Felton Road	D1-E1
Fresh Wharf Road	A1-B1
Gascoigne Road	B2-B1-C1
George Street	B3

Glenny Road	B4-C4
Gordon Road	D2
Greatfields Road	D1-D2
Harpour Road	B4
Harrow Road	D2-E2
Harts Lane	A4-B4-B3
Hertford Road	A2-A3
Highbridge Road	A1-A2
Howard Road	C1-C2-D2
Hulse Avenue	D4-E4-E3
Hurstbourne Gardens	D4-E4
Jackson Road	D1-D2
James Street	B3
Keith Road	D1
Kennedy Road	D1-D2
Keir Hardie Way	F3
King Edwards Road	C2-C1-D1
Lambourne Road	E2-E3
Lancaster Avenue	D2-D3
Levett Road	D4
Linton Road	B3
London Road	A2-A3-B3
Longbridge Road	C3-C4-D4
Loxford Road	A4-B4
Lyndhurst Gardens	D4-E4
Manor Road	E4-F4
Maybury Road	F1
Meadow Road	F3
Melford Avenue	E4
Melish Court	E1-E2
Morley Road	C2-D2
Movers Lane	D1-D2
Netherfield Gardens	C4-D4-D3
Norfolk Road	D3
North Street	B2-B3
Oakley Avenue	F4
Park Avenue	B4-C4
Perth Road	C1-D1
Priory Road	C3
Queens Road	B3-B4
Ripple Road	B3-C3-C2-D2-E2-F2
River Road	D1-E1
Rosslyn Road	C3-C4-D4
St Annes	B2-C2-C1
St Awdrys Road	C3-C2-D2
St Erkenwald Road	C2-C3
St Johns Road	D1-E1
St Margarets	C1
St Marys	C1
St Pauls Road	B2-C2
Sandringham Drive	E4
Salisbury Avenue	C3-D3-D4-E4
Sherwood Gardens	C4-C4-D3
Shirley Gardens	D4-E4
Sisley Road	E2-F2
Somerby Road	C3-C4
Sparsholt Road	D2-E2-E1
Strathfield Gardens	C4-D4
Stratton Drive	E4-F4
Sterry Road	E2
Suffolk Road	C3-D3-D2
Sunningdale Avenue	C2-C3
Surrey Road	D2-D3
Sutton Road	D1-E1
Tanner Street	B4
The Drive	E4-F4
The Shaftesburys	B1-C1
Thornhill Gardens	E3
Thorpe Road	C3

Town Quay	A2-B2
Tresham Road	E3
Upney Lane	E4-E3-F3-F2
Victoria Road	A4-B4
Wakering Road	B4-B3-C3
Wedderburn Road	D2
West Bank	A2
Westbury Road	C2
Westrow Drive	E4-F4
Wheelers Cross	C1
Whiting Avenue	A3-B3
Wilmington Gardens	C4-D4-D3-E3-E4

Stratford

Abbey Lane	A1
Abbey Road	B1
Aileen Walk	C2
Albert Square	C4
Aldworth Road	B2
Alma Street	A4-B4
Angel Lane	B3
Ash Road	C4
Atherton Road	C3-C4
Bridge Road	A2-B2-B1
Bridge Terrace	A2-B2
Broadway	B2-B3
Burford Road	A2-B2-B1
Buxton Road	B4-C4
Caistor Park Road	C1
Carnarvon Road	C3-C4
Carpenters Road	A1-A2
Cedars Road	C3
Chandos Road	A4-B4
Chant Street	B2
Chobham Road	A4-B4
Church Street	B1-C1
Cruickshank Road	C4
David Street	B4
Densham Road	B1-B2-C2
Devenay Road	C2
Earlham Grove	C4
Evesham Road	C2
Fairland Road	C3
Farringford Road	B2-C2
Forest Lane	B4-C4
Francis Street	B4
Geere Road	C1-C2
Glenavon Road	B3-C3-C2
Gibbins Road	A2
Great Eastern Road	A2-A3-B3
Grove Crescent Road	B3
Gurney Road	B4-C4
Ham Park Road	C2-C3
Harberson Road	C1
Hartland Road	C2
Heaton Place	A4
Henniker Road	A4-B4
High Street	A1-A2
Idmiston Road	C1
John Street	C1
Jupp Road	A2
Jupp Road West	A1-A2
Keogh Road	B3-C3-C4
Leyton Road	A4-A3-B3
Leytonstone Road	B4

Livingstone Road	A1
Louise Road	C3-C4
McGrath Road	C3-C4
Major Road	A4
Maneby Grove	B3
Maneby Street	B3-C3
Manor Road	C1
Maryland Park	B4
Maryland Road	B4
Maryland Street	B4
Meath Road	C1
Mortham Street	B1
New Plaistow Road	B1-C1
Paul Street	B1-B2
Pitchford Street	B2
Plaistow Road	C1
Portway	C2
Richford Road	C1-C2
Rokeby Street	B1-B2
Romford Road	B3-C3
St James Road	C4
Sandal Street	B1
Skiers Street	B1
Stephen's Road	B1-C1
Tavistock Road	C3
Temple Mill Lane	A4
Tennyson Road	B2-B3
The Green	C3
The Grove	B3
Union Street	A1
Vaughan Road	C3
Vicarage Lane	C2-C3
Victoria Street	B2
Waddington Road	B3-B4
Waddington Street	B3-B4
Warton Road	A1
Water Lane	B4-B3-C3
West Ham Lane	B1-B2
Willis Road	C1
Windmill Lane	B3
Wise Road	A1

East Ham

Aintree Avenue	A2-A3
Altmore Avenue	C2-C3-C4
Arthur Road	C1
Barking Road	A2-B2-C2
Bartle Avenue	B1-B2
Basil Avenue	A1
Bedford Road	C2-C3
Bendish Road	B4
Bridge Road	C4
Burgess Road	B4-C4
Caledon Road	B3-C3
Campbell Road	B2-B3
Caulfield Road	B3-C3
Central Park Road	A1-B1-B2
Cheltenham Gardens	A1
Clements Road	B4-C4
Colvin Road	A4-B4-B3
Cotswold Gardens	A1
Ernald Avenue	A2-A1-B1
Eversleigh Road	A4
Flanders Road	B1-C1
Friars Road	A2-A3
Geoffrey Gardens	A1

Gillett Avenue	A1-A2
Grangewood Street	A3
Grosvenor Road	A3
Haldane Road	A1
Hall Road	C2-C3
Harrow Road	B3-B4
Hartley Avenue	A2-A3
Heigham Road	A4-B4
Henniker Gardens	A1
Henry Road	B2
High Street North	B2-B3-B4
High Street South	B1-B2
Hockley Avenue	A1-A2
Holme Road	B3
Howard Road	C1
Katherine Road	A2-A3-A4
Kempton Road	B3
Keppel Road	B4-B3-C3-C2
Kimberley Avenue	A1-A2
Ladysmith Avenue	A1-A2
Lathom Road	B4-C4
Latimer Avenue	C2-C3
Lawrence Road	A4-B4
Lloyd Road	B2-C2
Mafeking Avenue	A1-A2
Malvern Road	A3
Market Street	B1-C1
Melbourne Road	C1-C2
Milton Avenue	A4-B4
Montpelier Gardens	A1
Napier Road	C1-C2
Navarre Road	B2
Nelson Street	B2-C2
Norfolk Road	C2-C3
Oakfield Road	A3-B3
Outram Road	A3-A4-B4
Phashet Grove	A4
Poulett Road	B2-C2
Pulleyns Avenue	A1-B1
Rancliffe Road	A1-B1
St Barts Road	B2
St Bernards Road	A2-A3
St Johns Road	A2-B2
Shoebury Road	C4
Sibley Grove	B4
Skeffington Road	B3-C3
Southend Road	B4-C4
Southchurch Road	B1-C1
Spencer Road	A3-A4
Stamford Road	A3-B3
Streatfield Avenue	C2-C3
Talbot Road	C1-C2
Thorpe Road	B3-C3
Tilbury Road	B1-C1
Victoria Avenue	A4
Wakefield Street	A3-B3
Wellington Road	C1-C2
Winter Avenue	B2-B3

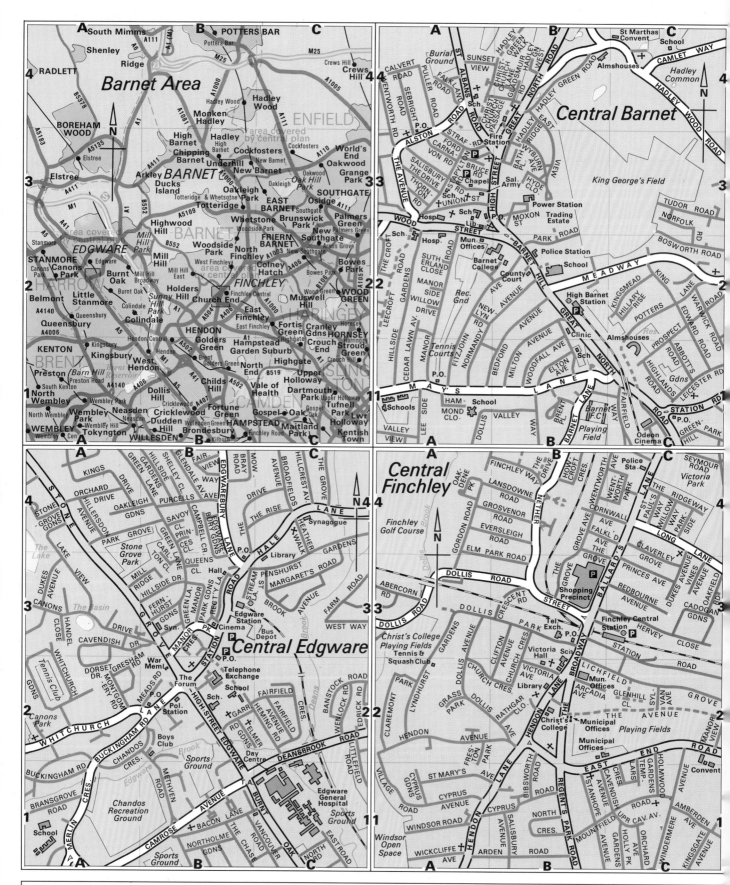

Barnet

Immortalised as the Cockney rhyming slang for 'hair', Barnet Fair started in the Middle Ages and is still held every year in September at Brent Lodge Farm, Mays Lane.

This was a fashionable residential area as early as the 18th century, and after the extension of the main line and underground railways in the late 19th and early 20th centuries, it developed into an important London borough. Long before this, its position on the Great North Road had made Barnet a popular staging post for coaches, and the High Street probably dates back to the 15th century. The Barnet Museum in Wood Street has an interesting local history collection.

Edgware lies on the line of Watling Street, the major Roman road which is roughly paralleled by the M1. Now mostly residential, Edgware was also at one time an important staging post. Several old buildings in the High Street date from that period, notably the White Hart, a 17th-century inn which has retained its covered wagon-way.

Finchley kept its country air until the late 19th century when it was heavily built on. The Bishop of London owned an extensive estate in this area during the 14th century, and despite intensive modernisation, Finchley still has several interesting quarters. The old parish church is in the Church End area.

Key to Town Plan and Area Plan

Town Plan

AA Recommended roads
Restricted roads
Other roads
Buildings of interest   Station ▣
Churches   ✝
Car Parks   ℗
Parks and open spaces

Area Plan

A roads
B roads
Stations   ●
Urban area
London Borough Boundary

Street Index with Grid Reference

Barnet

Abbott's Road	C1
Alston Road	A3-A4
Barnet Hill	B2
Barnet Lane	B1
Bath Place	B3
Bedford Avenue	A1-B1-B2
Bosworth Road	C3-C2
Brent Place	B1
Bruce Road	A3
Calvert Road	A4
Camlet Way	C4
Carnavon Road	A3
Cedar Lawn Avenue	A1-A2
Christchurch Lane	A4-B4
Christchurch Passage	A4
Dollis Valley Way	A1-B1
East View	B4-B3
Elton Avenue	B1
Fairfield Way	C1
Falkland Road	A4
Fitzjohn Avenue	A1-A2-B2
Gladsmuir Road	B4
Great North Road	B3-B4,C1-B1-B2
Greenhill Park	C1
Hadley Green Road	B4
Hadley Green Walk	B4
Hadley Green West	B4
Hadley Ridge	B3-B4
Hadley Wood Road	C3-C4
Hammond Close	A1
Highlands Road	C1
High Street	B3-A3
Hillary Rise	C2
Hillside Gardens	A1-A2-A3
Hyde Close	B3
King Edward Road	C2-C1
Kingsmead	C2
Leecroft Road	A1-A2-A3
Lee Side	A1
Leicester Road	C1
Manor Road	A1-A2-A3
Manor Side	A2

May's Lane	A1-B1-C1
Meadway	B2-C2
Milton Avenue	B1-B2
Moxon Street	B3
Newlyn Road	A2
Norfolk Road	C3-C2
Normandy Avenue	A1-A2-B2
Park Road	B2-B3
Potters Lane	C1-C2
Prospect Road	C1-C2
Puller Road	A4
St Albans Road	A4-A3-B3
Salisbury Road	A3
Sebright Avenue	A4-A3
Stapylton Road	A3
Station Road	C1
Strafford Road	A3
Sunset View	A4-B4
Sutherland Close	A2
The Avenue	A3
The Croft	A2
The Drive	A3
Thornton Road	A3
Tudor Road	C3
Union Street	A3
Valley View	A1
Warwick Road	C2-C1
Wentworth Road	A4-A3
Willow Drive	A2
Woodfall Avenue	B1-B2
Wood Street	A3-A2-B3-B2
Wyburn Avenue	B3

Edgeware

Bacon Lane	B1-C1
Banstock Road	C2
Bransgrove Road	A1
Broadfields Avenue	C4
Buckingham Road	A1-A2-B2
Burnt Oak	B1-C1
Carlton Close	B4-B3
Campbell Crescent	B4
Camrose Avenue	A1-B1
Canons Drive	A3-B3
Cavendish Drive	A3-B3
Chandos Crescent	A1-A2-B2
Deansbrook Road	B1-C1-C2
Dorset Drive	A2-A3
Dukes Avenue	A3
East Road	C1
Edgewarebury Gardens	B4-B3
Edgewarebury Lane	B4-B3
Edrick Road	C2
Elmer Gardens	B2-C2
Fairfield Avenue	C2
Fairfield Crescent	B2-C2
Fairview Way	B4
Farm Road	C3
Fernhurst Gardens	B3
Garratt Road	B2
Glendale Avenue	B4
Green Lane	A4-B4-B3
Gresham Road	A2
Hale Lane	B3-B4-C3-C4
Handel Close	A3
Hark Grove	A4-B4
Heather Walk	C4
Heming Road	B2-C2
High Street Edgeware	B2-B1

Hillcrest Avenue	C4
Hillersdon Avenue	A4
Hillside Drive	B3
Hillside Gardens	B4
Kings Drive	A4
Lake View	A4-A3
Littlefield Road	C2-C1
Manor Park Crescent	B3
Manor Park Gardens	B3
Margaret's Road	C3-C4
Meads Road	B2
Merlin Crescent	A1-A2
Methven Road	B2-B1
Mill Ridge	A3-B3
Montgomery Road	A2
Mowbray Road	B4
Northolme Gardens	B1
North Road	C1
Oakleigh Gardens	A4-B4
Orchard Drive	A4
Park Grove	A4-B4
Penhurst Gardens	B3-C3-C4
Princes Close	B4
Purcells Avenue	B4
Queens Close	B3
Rectory Lane	B3
St Brook Avenue	C3
Savoy Close	B4
Shelley Close	B4
Station Road	B2-B3
Stone Grove	A4-A3-B3-B2
Stonegrove Gardens	A4
Stream Lane	B3
The Chase	B1-C1
The Drive	B4-C4
The Grove	C4
The Rise	B4-C4
Vancouver Road	B1-C1
Wenlock Road	C2
West Way	C3
Whitchurch Gardens	A2-A3
Whitchurch Lane	A2-B2

Finchley

Abercorn Road	A3
Amberden Avenue	C1
Arcadia Avenue	B2
Arden Road	A1-B1
Ballard's Lane	B3-C3-C4
Bibsworth Road	B1-B2
Cadogan Gardens	C3
Cavendish Avenue	B1-C1
Church Crescent	A2-B2-B3
Claremont Park	A2
Claverley Grove	C4-C3
Clifton Avenue	B2-B3
Cornwall Avenue	B4-C4
Crescent Road	B3
Cyprus Avenue	A1
Cyprus Gardens	A1
Cyprus Road	A1-B1
Dollis Avenue	A3-A2-B2
Dollis Park	A3-B3
Dollis Road	A3-B3
Dukes Avenue	C3-C4
East End Road	B1-B2-C1-C2
Elm Park Road	A4-A3-B3
Eversleigh Road	A4-B4
Falkland Avenue	B4-C4

Finchley Way	A4-B4
Freston Park	A1-A2
Glenhill Close	C2
Gordon Road	A3-A4
Grass Park	A2
Grosvenor Road	A4-B4
Grove Avenue	B4
Hendon Avenue	A2-B2
Hendon Lane	A1-B1-B2
Hervey Close	B3-C3
Holly Park Gardens	C1
Holmwood Gardens	C2-C1
Howcroft Crescent	B4
Kingsgate Avenue	C1
Lansdowne Road	A4-B4
Lichfield Grove	B3-B2-C2
Long Lane	C4-C3
Lyndhurst Gardens	A2-A3
Manor View	C2
Mountfield Road	B1-C1
Nether Street	B4-B3
North Crescent	B1
Oakdene Park	A4
Oakfield Road	C3
Orchard Avenue	C1
Parkside	C4
Princes Avenue	C3
Rathgar Close	B2
Redbourne Avenue	C3
Regent's Park Road	B1
St Mary's Avenue	A1-B1
St Paul's Way	C4
Salisbury Avenue	B1
Seymour Road	C4
Stanhope Avenue	B1-C1
Station Road	B3-C3-C2
Sylvan Avenue	C2
The Avenue	B2-C2
The Broadway	B2-B3
The Drive	B4
The Grove	B3-B4-C3
The Ridgeway	C4
Templars Crescent	C2-C1
Upper Canendish Avenue	C1
Victoria Avenue	B2
Village Road	A1-A2
Vines Avenue	C3
Wentworth Avenue	B4-C4
Wentworth Park	B4-C4
Wickcliffe Avenue	A1
Willow Way	C4
Windermere Avenue	C1-C2
Windsor Road	A1

BARNET
The Parish Church of St James, Friern Barnet, on the eastern side of the borough. Although part of London, Barnet reaches out into open country and still has distinct village communities.

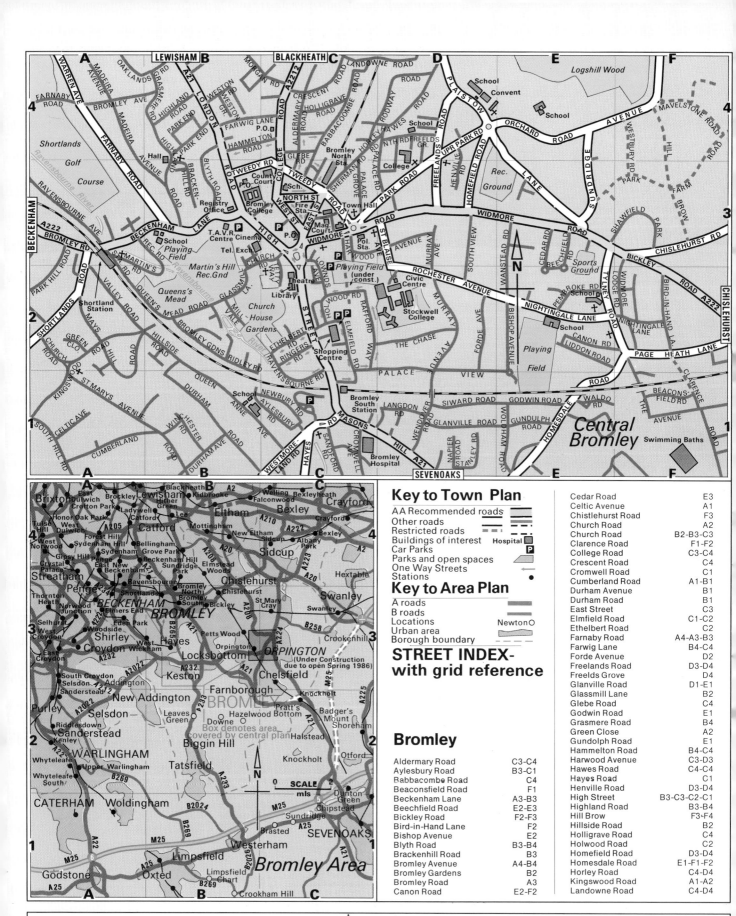

Key to Town Plan

AA Recommended roads	
Other roads	
Restricted roads	
Buildings of interest	Hospital
Car Parks	P
Parks and open spaces	
One Way Streets	
Stations	●

Key to Area Plan

A roads	
B roads	
Locations	Newton○
Urban area	
Borough boundary	

STREET INDEX- with grid reference

Bromley

Aldermary Road	C3-C4
Aylesbury Road	B3-C1
Babbacombe Road	C4
Beaconsfield Road	F1
Beckenham Lane	A3-B3
Beechfield Road	E2-E3
Bickley Road	F2-F3
Bird-in-Hand Lane	F2
Bishop Avenue	E2
Blyth Road	B3-B4
Brackenhill Road	B3
Bromley Avenue	A4-B4
Bromley Gardens	B2
Bromley Road	A3
Canon Road	E2-F2

Cedar Road	E3
Celtic Avenue	A1
Chistlehurst Road	F3
Church Road	A2
Church Road	B2-B3-C3
Clarence Road	F1-F2
College Road	C3-C4
Crescent Road	C4
Cromwell Road	C1
Cumberland Road	A1-B1
Durham Avenue	B1
Durham Road	B1
East Street	C3
Elmfield Road	C1-C2
Ethelbert Road	C2
Farnaby Road	A4-A3-B3
Farwig Lane	B4-C4
Forde Avenue	D2
Freelands Road	D3-D4
Freelds Grove	D4
Glanville Road	D1-E1
Glassmill Lane	B2
Glebe Road	C4
Godwin Road	E1
Grasmere Road	B4
Green Close	A2
Gundolph Road	E1
Hammelton Road	B4-C4
Harwood Avenue	C3-D3
Hawes Road	C4-C4
Hayes Road	C1
Henville Road	D3-D4
High Street	B3-C3-C2-C1
Highland Road	B3-B4
Hill Brow	F3-F4
Hillside Road	B2
Holligrave Road	C4
Holwood Road	C2
Homefield Road	D3-D4
Homesdale Road	E1-F1-F2
Horley Road	C4-D4
Kingswood Road	A1-A2
Landowne Road	C4-D4

Bromley

Birthplace of H G Wells, Bromley is thought by some to be one of the most favoured residential areas to the south of London. It has an abundance of trees and parks, and even in the centre, Queens Garden and Church House Gardens form quiet oases. In spite of development this century, Bromley has kept many of its older buildings, Bromley Palace and Bromley College among them. The house in which H G Wells was born no longer stands, but a plaque marks its site in the High Street. At Norman Park, Bromley also boasts an excellent all-weather running track.

Beckenham Development in the 1920s and 1930s left few of the older buildings standing except in a small area near the High Street, but Beckenham's tree-lined roads and numerous parks are compensation for this. Kelsey Park, in the town centre, is a beautiful expanse of woods, lawns, flowers and a stream.

Orpington's history can be traced back to the Stone Age, but ironically it was the last of the major areas of the borough to be developed. When it came, in the 1930s and later, development included such innovations as The Walnuts, a town centre shopping precinct, Civic Centre and sports hall. Reminders of the town's past still survive, and the London Borough of Bromley Priory Museum, in Church Hill, has interesting exhibits.

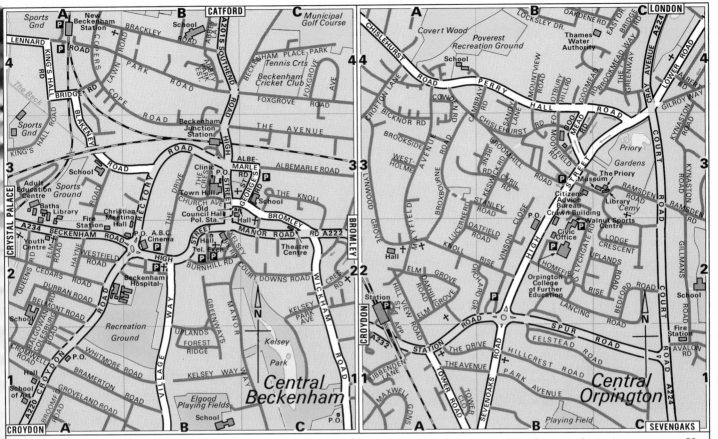

Central Beckenham

Central Orpington

Langdon Road	D1	Valley Road	A2
Liddon Road	E2	Waldo Road	E1
London Road	B3-B4	Wanstead Road	E2-E3
Lownds Avenue	C2-C3	Warren Avenue	A4
Madeira Avenue	A4-A3-B3	Wendover Road	D1
Martins Road	A3-A2-B2	West Street	C3
Masons Hill	C1-D1	Westbury Road	F3-F4
Mavelstone Road	F4	Westmoreland Road	C1
Mays Hill Road	A1-A2	Weston Grove	B4
Mill Vale	B2	Weston Road	B4
Morgan Road	B4-C4	Widmore Road	C3-D3-E3
Murray Avenue	D1-D2-D3	Widmore Lodge Road	F2-F3
Napier Road	D1	Winchester Road	B1
Newbury Road	B1-C1	Woldham Road	E1
Nightingale Lane	E2-F2		
North Road	D4		
North Street	C3		
Oaklands Road	A4-B4		
Orchard Road	D4-E4		
Page Heath Lane	F2	**Beckenham**	
Palace Grove	C3		
Palace Road	D3-D4		
Palace View	C2-D2-E2	Abbey Lane	B4
Park End	D3	Abbey Park Estate	B4
Park Road	C3-D3	Albemarle Road	B3-C3
Park Farm Road	E3-F3-F4	Balgowan Road	A1-A2
Park Hill Road	A2-A3	Beckenham Road	A3-A2-B2
Pembroke Road	E2	Beckenham Place Park	B4-C4
Plaistow Lane	D4-E4-E3	Belmont Road	A2
Queen Anne Avenue	B2-B1-C1	Blakeney Road	A4-A3-B3
Queen's Mead Road	A2-B2	Brackley Road	A4-B4
Rafford Way	C2	Bramerton Road	A1-B1
Ravensbourne Avenue	A3	Bridge Road	A4
Ravensbourne Road	C1-C2	Bromley road	C2-C3
Recreation Road	A3-B3	Broomfield Road	A1
Ridley Road	B1-B2	Burnhill Road	B2
Ringers Road	C2	Cedars Road	A2
Rochester Avenue	D3-D2-E2	Church Avenue	B3
Rodway Road	C4-D4	Colesburg Road	A1-A2
St Blaise Avenue	D2-D3	Copers Cope Road	A4-B4-B3
St Marys Avenue	A1-B1	Court Downs Road	C2
Sandford Road	C1	Crescent Road	C2
Shawfield Park	E3-F3	Cromwell Road	A1
Sherman Road	C3-C4	Croydon Road	A1-A2-B2
Shorlands Road	A2-A3	Durbon Road	A2
Siwood Road	D1-E1	Elm Road	A2
South View	D2-D3	Forest Ridge	B1
South Hill Road	A1	Foxgrove Avenue	C4
Stanley Road	D1	Foxgrove Road	C4
Station Road	A2-A3	Greenways Road	B1-B2
Sundridge Avenue	E3-E4-F4	Hayne Road	A2-A3
Tetty Way	C2-C3	High Street	B2-B3
The Avenue	F1	Kelsey Way	B1-C1
The Chase	D2	Kelsey Park Avenue	C1-C2
Tweedy Road	B3-C3-C4	Kelsey Park Road	B2
Tylney Road	E3-E2-F2	King's Hall Road	A3-A4
Upper Park Road	D4	Lawn Road	A4-B4

Lennard Road	A4	Lodge Crescent	C2
Manor Road	B2-C2	Lower Road	C4
Manor Way	C2-B2-C2-C1	Lucerne Road	A2-A3
Park Road	A4-B4	Lychgate Road	B2-B3
Queens Road	A2	Lynwood Grove	A2-A3
Rectory Road	B2-B3	Maxwell Gardens	A1
St George's Road	C3	Mayfield Avenue	A2-A3-A4
Southend Road	B3-B4	Moorfield Road	B3
The Avenue	B3-C3	Mountview Road	B4
The Crescent	B3	Oakdene Road	B4-C4
The Drive	B2-B3	Oakhill Road	A2
The Knoll	C2-C3	Oatfield Road	A2-B2
Uplands	B1	Orchard Grove	B2
Village Way	B1-B2	Park Avenue	B1-C1
Westfield Road	A2	Perry Hall Road	A4-B4-C4-C3
Whitmore Road	A1-B1	Ramsden Road	C2-C3
Wickham Road	C1-C2	Sandy Lane	B3-B4
		Sevenoaks Road	B1
		Spur Road	B2-B1-C1
		Stanley Road	A3-B3
Orpington		Station Approach	A1-A2
		Station Road	A1-A2-B2
		The Avenue	A1-B1
Albert Road	C4	The Drive	A1-B1
Avalon Road	C1	The Greenway	C4
Bedford Road	C2	Tower Close	A1
Bicknor Road	A3-A4	Tower Road	A1
Brookmead Way	C4	Tubbenden Lane	A1
Brookside	A3	Uplands Road	B2-C2
Broomhill Road	B3	Vinson Close	B2-B3
Broxbourne Road	A2-A3	Westholme	A3
Cambray Road	B3-B4		
Chislehurst Road	A4-A3-B3		
Court Road	C1-C2-C3		
Cowden Road	A3-A4		
Cray Avenue	C4		
Crofton Lane	A3-A4		
Cyril Road	B3		
East Drive	C4		
Elm Grove	A2		
Felstead Road	B1-C1		
Footbury Hill Road	B3-B4		
Gillmans Road	C1-C2-C3		
Gilroy Way	C4		
Goomead Road	B3-B4-C4		
High Street	B2-B3-C3		
Hillcrest Road	B1-C1		
Hill View Road	A1-A2		
Homefield Rise	B2-C2		
Irene Road	B3		
Keswick Road	B3		
Knoll Rise	A2-B3		
Kynaston Road	C3-C4		
Lancing Road	B2-C2		
Locksley Drive	B4		

Central London

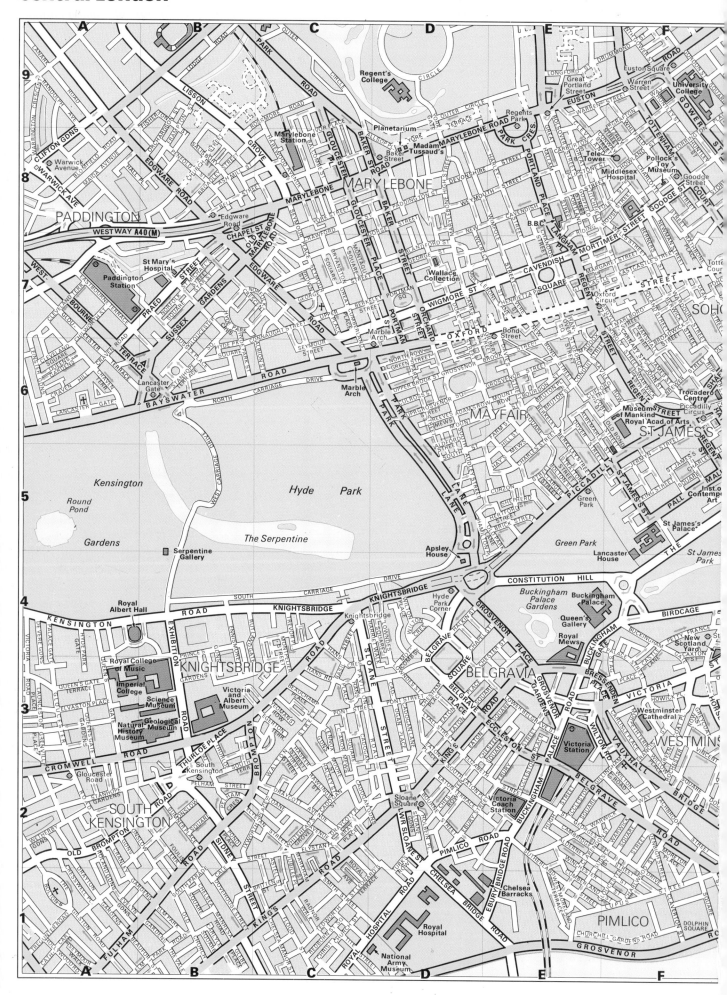

Key to Town Plan

Town Plan

AA Recommended roads
Restricted roads
Other roads
Buildings of interest Cinema
Car Parks P
Churches
Parks and open spaces
Underground Stations
One Way Streets

Street Index with Grid Reference

Central London

Abingdon Street G3-G4
Adams Row D6-E6
Albany Road K1-L1
Albert Embankment H1-H2-H3
Albermarle Street E6-E5-F5-F6
Alberta Street J2
Albion Street C6
Aldridge Street L2
Alderney Street E2-F2-F1
Aldergate Street J7-K7-K6
Aldford Street D5-D6
Aldwych H6-H7-I7
Allsop Place C8-D8
Alsey Street C2
Amelia Street J2-K2
Appold Street L8-L9
Argyll Street E7-F7
Ashmill Street B8-C8
Astell Street C1-C2
Atterbury Street G2
Aylesford Street G1
Baker Street C8-D8-D7
Balcombe Street C8
Baldwins Gardens I8
Balfour Street K2-K3
Bankside J6-K6
Banner Street K9
Barbican J8
Basil Street C3-C4
Basinghall Street K7-K8
Bath Terrace K3-K4
Baylis Road I4
Bayswater Road A6-B6-C6
Beauchamp Place C3
Beak Street F6
Bear Lane J5
Beaufort Street A1-B1
Bedford Avenue G8
Bedford Place G8
Bedford Square F8-G8
Bedford Walk G9
Beech Street J8-K8
Belgrave Place D3
Belgrave Road E3-E2-F2
Belgrave Square D3-D4
Bell Street B8-C8
Bell Yard I7
Belvedere Street H4-H5
Berkeley Square E6
Berkeley Street C7-D7
Berkeley Street E5-E6
Bermondsey Street L4-L5
Berners Street F7-F8
Berwick Street F6-F7
Birdcage Walk F4-G4
Bishopsgate L7-L8
Blackfriars Bridge J6
Blackfriars Road J4-J5
Black Prince Road H2-I2
Blandford Street D7
Blomfield Road A8
Bloomsbury Street G7-G8
Bloomsbury Way G8-H8
Bolsover Street E8-E9
Bolton Street E5
Borough High Street K4-K5-J5
Borough Road J4-K4
Boswell Street H8
Bourdon Street E6
Bourne Street D2
Bouverie Street I7
Bowling Green Lane I9
Bow Street H7
Braganza Street J1-J2
Brandon Street K2-K3
Bray Place C2
Bressenden Place E3-F3
Brewer Street F6
Brick Street E5
Bridge Street G4-H4
Britten Street B1-C1
Broadley Street B8
Broadwick Street F6-F7
Brompton Road C2-B2-B3-C3-C4
Brook Drive I3-J3
Brook Street D6-E6-E7
Browning Street K2
Brown Street C7
Brunswick Square G9-H9
Bruton Place E6
Bruton Street E6
Bryanston Square C7
Buckingham Gate E3-E4-F4-F3
Buckingham Palace Road E2-E3
Bunhill Row K8-K9
Cadiz Street K1-K2
Cadogan Gardens C2-D2
Cadogan Lane D3
Cadogan Place D3
Cadogan Street C2
Cadogan Square C2-C3
Cale Street B1-B2-C2
Calthorpe Street H9-I9
Cambridge Street E2-F2-F1
Cannon Street J7-K7-K6-L6
Cardigan Street I1-I2
Carey Street H7-I7
Carlisle Lane I3-I4
Carlisle Place F3
Carlyle Square B1
Carnaby Street F6-F7
Carter Lane J7-K7
Carter Road J1-K1
Castle Lane F3-F4
Cathcart Road A1
Cavendish Square E7
Caxton Street F4
Chancery Lane I7-I8
Chandos Place G6
Chandos Street E7-E8
Chapel Street D4-E4
Chapel Street B7-B8-C8
Charing Cross Road G6-G7
Charles Street E5-E6
Charles II Street F5-F6-G6
Charlotte Street F8
Charlwood Street F1-F2
Charterhouse Street J8
Charter Road J1
Chatham Street K3-L3
Cheapside K7
Chelsea Bridge Road D2-D1-E1
Chelsea Manor Street C1
Chelsea Square B1
Chesham Place D3
Chester Row D2
Chester Square D3-E3-E2
Chester Street D3-D4-E4-E3
Chilworth Street A6-A7
Chiswell Street K8-L8
Christchurch Street C1
Church Street B8
Churchill Gardens Road E1-F1
City Road K9-L9-L8
Clabon Mews C2-C3
Clarendon Street E2-F2
Clarges Street E5
Claverton Street F1
Clayton Street I1
Clerkenwell Road I8-I9-J9
Cleveland Square A6
Cleveland Street E9-E8-F8
Cleveland Terrace A7
Clifford Street E6-F6
Clifton Gardens A8
Clifton Street L8-L9
Clink Street K5-K6
Clipstone Street E8-F8
Cock Lane J8
Coin Street I5
Coleman Street K7-K8
Cole Street K4
Compton Street J8
Conduit Street E6-E7
Congreve Street L2-L3
Connaught Street B6-B7-C7-C6
Constitution Hill E4-F4
Conway Street E8-F8
Cook's Road J1
Copperfield Street J5-K5
Cork Street E6-F6
Cornhill K7-L7
Cornwall Road I4-I5
Cosser Street I3
County Street K3
Courtenay Street I1-I2
Courtfield Road A2
Covent Garden G6-H6-H7
Coventry Street F6-G6
Cowan Street L1
Cowcross Street J8
Crampton Street J2-K2
Cranley Gardens A2-A1-B1
Craven Hill A6
Craven Terrace A6
Crawford Street C7-C8-D8
Cresswell Place A1-A2
Cromwell Road A2-A3-B3
Cullcross Street D6
Cumberland Street E2-E1-F1
Curtain Road L9
Curzon Street D5-E5-E6
Dante Road J2-J3
Darwin Street L3
Date Street K2
Davies Street E6-E7
Dawes Street L2
Deacon Way K3
Dean Street F7-G7
Decima Street L4
Delaune Street J1-J2
Denbigh Street F1-F2
Devere Gardens A3-A4
Deverell Street K3-L3
Devonshire Street D8-E8
Doddington Grove J1
Dolben Street J5
Dolphin Square F1
Dorset Street C7-C8-D8
Doughty Street H9
Douglas Street F2-G2
Dovehouse Street B1
Dover Street E5-E6
Downing Street G5
Draycott Avenue C2
Draycott Place C2
Drayton Gardens A1-A2
Drummond Street E9-F9
Dufferin Street K9
Duke Street D7
Durham Street H1
Dury Lane G7-H7
Eastbourne Terrace A7
East Castle Street F7
Eastcheap L6
East Street K2-L2
Eaton Place D3
Eaton Square D3-E3
Eaton Terrace D2
Eccleston Place E2-E3
Eccleston Square E2
Eccleston Street E3
Ebury Bridge Road D1-E1-E2
Ebury Street D2-E2-E3
Edgware Road A8-B8-B7-C7-C6
Egerton Terrace C3
Eldon Street L8
Elizabeth Street D3-D2-E2
Elliots Row J3
Elm Park Gardens B1
Elm Park Road A1-B1
Elsted Street L2
Elvaston Place A3
Elystan Place C2
Elystan Street B2-C2
Emerson Street K5-K6
Endell Street G7-H7
Ennismore Gardens B3-B4
Epworth Street L9
Erasmus Street G2
Euston Road E9-F9
Evelyn Gardens A1-B1
Ewer Street J5
Exhibition Road B3-B4
Exmouth Market I9
Falmouth Road K3-K4
Fann Street J8-J9-K9-K8
Faringdon Road I9
Farm Street D6-E6
Farringdon Road I8-J8
Farringdon Street J7-J8
Fenchurch Street L6-L7
Fielding Street K1
Finsbury Circus L8
Finsbury Square L8-L9
First Street C2-C3
Fisherton Street A9-B9-B8
Fitzalen Street I8
Fitzroy Street F8-F9
Fleet Street I7-J7
Fleming Road J1
Flint Street L2
Flood Street C1
Floral Street G6-G7-H7
Foley Street E8-F8
Fore Street K8
Foulis Terrace B2
Frampton Street B8-B9
Frazer Street I4
Frith Street G7
Fulham Road A1-B1-B2
Gee Street J9
George Street C7-D7
Gerrard Street G6
Gilbert Road I2-I3-J3
Gilbert Street D7-D6-E6
Gillingham Street E2-F2-F3
Gilston Road A1
Giltspur Street J7-J8
Glasshouse Walk H2
Glebe Place B1
Gloucester Place C9-C8-C7-D7
Gloucester Road A2-A3
Gloucester Square B6-B7
Gloucester Street E1-F1-F2
Gloucester Terrace A6-A7
Goodge Street F8
Golden Lane K8-K9
Gordon Square F9-G9
Gordon Street F9
Gossfield Street E8
Goswell Road J8-J9
Gough Street H9-I9
Gower Street F9-F8-G8
Gracechurch Street L6-L7
Grafton Way F9
Gray's Inn Road H9-I9-I8
Great Castle Street E7-F7
Great Cumberland Place C6-C7
Great Dover Street K4-K3-L3
Great George Street G4
Great Guildford Street J5-K5
Great Marlborough Street F7
Great Ormond Street H8-H9
Great Peter Street F3-G3
Great Portland Street E7-E8-E9
Great Russel Street F7-F8-G8
Great Smith Street G3-G4
Great Suffolk Street J4-J5
Great Titchfield Street E8-E7-F7
Greek Street G7
Greencoat Place F3
Green Street D6
Gresham Street K7
Greville Street I8
Greycoat Street F3
Grosvenor Gardens E3
Grosvenor Place D4-E4-E3
Grosvenor Road E1-F1-G1
Grosvenor Square D6
Grosvenor Street D6-E6
Guilford Street G9-H9
Guy Street L4
Halkin Street D4
Hallam Street E8
Hall Place A8-B8
Hamilton Place D4-D5-E5-E4
Hanover Square E7
Hans Crescent C3-C4
Hans Place C3
Hans Road C3
Harewood Avenue C8-C9
Harley Ford Road H1
Harley Street D8-E8-E7
Harper Road K3-K4
Harriet Walk C4-D4-D3
Harrington Gardens A2
Hasker Street C2-C3
Hatfields I5-J5
Hatton Garden I8
Hayle Street J3
Haymarket F6-G6-G5
Hay's Mews E5-E6
Henrietta Place E7
Hercules Road I3-I4
Hertford Street D5-E5
Heygate Street K2-K3
High Holborn G7-H7-H8-I8
Hill Street E5-E6
Holbein Place D2
Holborn H8-I8
Holborn Circus I8
Holborn Viaduct I8-J8-J7
Holland Street J5-J6
Hollywood Road A1
Holyoake Road J2-J3
Hopton Street J5-J6
Horseferry Road F3-G3
Horse Guards Road G4-G5
House Street E8-F8
Howick Place F3
Howland Street F8
Hugh Street E2
Huntley Street F8-F9
Hyde Park Crescent B7
Hyde Park Gate A3-A4
Hyde Park Square B6
Hyde Park Street B6-B7
Innfields H7-I7
Ivor Place C8-C9
Ixworth Place B2-C2
James Street D7
James Street F6
Jermyn Street F5-F6
Jockey's Fields H8
John Adams Street G6-H6
Johnathan Street H2
John Islip Street G2-G3
John Street F6
John Street J9
Jubilee Place C1-C2
Kempsford Road I2-J2
Kennington Lane I2-J2
Kennington Park I1-J1
Kennington Park Road I1-J1-J2
Kennington Road I1-I2-I3
Kensington Road A4-B4
King Charles Street G4
King James Street J4
Kingslake Street L1-L2
Kingly Street F6-F7
King's Road B1-C1-C2-D2-D3-E3
King Street F5
Kingsway H7-H8
King William Street K7-L7-L6
Kipling Street L4-L5
Knightsbridge B4-C4-D4
Lambeth Bridge G3-H3
Lambeth High Street H2-H3
Lambeth Palace Road H3-H4
Lambeth Road H3-I3-I4-J4
Lambeth Walk I3
Lanark Gate A9
Lancaster Gate A6
Langham Place E7-E8
Langle Lane H1
Lant Street K4
Larcom Street K2
Launceston Place A3
Lavington Street J5
Lawn Lane H1
Law Street L3-L4
Leadenhall Street L7
Leather Lane I8-I9
Leather Market Street L4
Leicester Square G6
Leinster Gardens A6-A7
Lennox Gardens C3
Leonard Street L9
Lincoln's H7-H8
Lisle Street G6
Lisson Grove B8-C8
Liverpool Grove K1-K2
Lodge Road B9
Lollard Street H3-I3-I2
Lombard Street K7-L7
London Bridge L5-L6
London Road J2-J3
London Wall K8-L8-L7
Long Acre G6-G7-H7
Longford Street E9
Long Lane J8
Long Lane K4-L4
Lorrimore Road J1
Lower Belgrave Street E3
Lower Marsh I4
Lower Sloane Street D2
Lower Thames Street L6
Lowndes Square D4
Lowndes Street D3
Ludgate Hill J7
Luke Street L9
Lupus Street E1-F1
Lyall Street D3
Maddox Street E6-E7
Maida Avenue A8
Maiden Lane G6-H6
Malet Street F9-G9-G8
Manciple Street K4-L4
Manresa Road B1
Manor Place J1-J2-K2
Marchmont Street G9
Marcia Road L2
Margaret Street E7-F7
Markham Street C1-C2
Marshall Street F6-F7
Marshalsea Road K4-K5
Marsham Street G2-G3
Marylebone High Street D7-D8
Marylebone Lane D7-E7
Marylebone Road B8-C8-D8-D9-E9
Mecklenburgh Square H9
Medway Street G3
Melton Street F9
Merrow Street K1-L1-L2
Methley Street I1-I2
Milk Street K7
Millbank G2-G3
Millman Street H9
Mint Street J4
Monk Street G3
Monmouth Street G6-G7
Montague Place G8
Montford Place I1
Montague Street G8
Montagu Square C7
Montpelier Street C3-C4
Moorfields K8
Moore Street C2-C3
Moorgate K7-K8-L8
Morecambe Street K2
Moreton Place F2
Mortimer Street E7-F7-F8
Morley Street I4
Morpeth Terrace F3
Motcomb Street D3-D4
Mount Row E6
Munton Road K3
Museum Street G7-G8
Neal Street G7
New Bond Street E6-E7
New Bridge Street J6-J7
New Cavendish Street D8-E8-F8
New Change K7
Newcomen Street K5-L5
New Compton Street G7
Newgate Street J7
Newington Butts J2-J3
Newington Causeway J3-J4-K4
New Kent Road J3-K3-L3
Newman Street F7-F8
New Oxford Street G7-G8
Newton Street H7-H8
Nine Elms Lane G1
Norfolk Crescent B7-C7
Norfolk Square B7
North Carriage Drive B6-C6
North Gower Street F9
Northington Street H8-I9
Northumberland Avenue G5-H5
North Row D6
Old Bailey J7
Old Bond Street E6-F6-F5
Old Broad Street L7-L8
Old Brompton Road A1-A2-B2
Old Compton Street F6-G6-G7
Old Marylebone Road B7-C7-C8
Old Park Lane D5-E5
Old Pye Street F3-G3
Old Street J9-K9-L9
Olney Road J1-K1
Onslow Gardens A2-B2
Onslow Square B2
Oswin Street G3
Ontario Street J3-J4
Orb Street K2
Orchardson Street B8-B9
Orchard Street D7
Outer Circle C9-D9-D8-D9-E9
Oval Way H1-I1
Oxford Street D6-D7-E7-F7
Paddington Street D8
Page Street G3
Pages Walk L3
Palace Gate A3-A4
Palace Street E4-F4-F3
Pall Mall F5-G5
Pardoner Street L4
Paris Garden J5
Park Crescent E8-E9
Park Lane C6-D6-D5-D4
Park Road B9-C9
Park Street J5-J6
Parry Street G1-H1
Paul Street L9
Pavilion Road C4-C3-D3-D2
Pearman Street I4
Pelham Crescent B2
Pelham Street B2
Penfold Street B8
Penrose Street K1-J1-K1-K2
Penton Place J2-K2
Piccadilly E4-E5-F5-F6
Pilgrimage Street K4
Pimlico Road D2-E2
Pocock Street J4-J5
Poland Street F7
Pond Place B2
Ponsonby Place G2
Pont Street C3-D3
Porchester Terrace A6
Portland Place E8
Portland Street K2-K1-L1
Portman Square D7
Portman Street D6-D7
Portugal Street H7
Poultry K7
Praed Street A7-B7
Prince's Gardens B3-B4
Queens Gardens A6
Queen's Gate A3-A4
Queens Gate Gardens A3
Queen's Gate Terrace A3
Queen Square G8-G9-H9-H8
Queen Street K6-K7
Queen Victoria Street J7-J6-K6-K7
Radnor Walk C1
Randolph Avenue A8-A9
Rathbone Place F7-F8
Rawlings Street C2
Redburn Street C1
Redcross Way K5
Red Lion Street H8
Reeves Mews D6
Regency Street G2-G3
Regent Street E7-F7-F6-F5-G5
Renfrew Road J2-J3
Rivington Street L9
Rothsay Street L3-L4
Rochester Row F2-F3
Rockingham Street J3-K3
Rodney Road K3-K2-L2
Roland Gardens A1-A2
Romilly Street G6-G7
Rossmore Road B8-B9-C9
Roupell Street I5-J5
Royal Avenue C1-C2
Royal Hospital Road C1-D1-D2
Royal Street H4-I4
Rupert Street F6-G6
Russell Square G8-G9
Rutland Gate B4-B3-C3
St George's Drive E2-F2-F1
St Georges Road I4-I3-J3
St George's Square F1-G1
St George Street E6-E7
St Giles High Street G7
St James Square F5
St James's Street F5
St John Street J8-J9
St Leonard's Terrace C1-D1-D2
St Martin's Lane G6
St Mary Axe L7
St Michael's Street B7
St Thomas Street K5-L5
Saffron Hill I8-I9
Salisbury Street B8
Sancroft Street H2-I2
Savile Row E6-F6
Savoy Place H6
Scritton Street L9
Sekforde Street J9
Seymour Place C7-C8
Seymour Street C6-C7
Seymour Walk A1
Shaftesbury Avenue F6-G6-G7
Shelton Street G7
Shepherd Street E5
Shoe Lane I7-J7
Sidney Street B2-B1-C1
Silk Street K8
Skinner Street I9-J9
Sloane Avenue C2
Sloane Gardens D2
Sloane Street C4-C3-D3-D2
Smith Square G3
Smith Street C1
Snows Fields L5
Soho Square F7
Southampton Row G8
South Audley Street D5-D6
South Carriage Drive B4-C4-D4
South Eaton Place D2-D3
South Parade B1-B2
South Terrace B2-B3
Southwark Bridge K6
Southwark Bridge Road J3-J4-K4-K5
Southwark Street J5-K5
Stag Place F3-F4
Stamford Street I5-J5
Stanhope Gardens A2
Stanhope Terrace B
Stannary Street I
Star Street B
Stead Street K
Store Street F8-G
Strand G5-G6-H6-H
Stratton Street E
Sturgeon Road J
Sumner Place B
Sumner Street J5-K
Sun Street L
Surrey Square L
Sussex Gardens A6-B6-B
Sussex Place B6-B
Sussex Street E2-F
Sutherland Street E1-E
Sutherland Walk K
Tabard Street K4-L4-L
Tabernacle Street L
Tachbrook Street F
Tavistock Square G
Tavistock Street H6-H
Tedworth Square C
Temple Avenue I6-I
The Boltons A1-A
The Cut I4-I5-J
Theed Street I
The Little Boltons A
The Mall F4-F5-G
Theobald's Road H8-I
The Vale B
Threadneedle Street K7-L
Throgmorton Street K7-L
Thurloe Place B2-B
Thurloe Square B2-B
Thurloe Street L1-L
Tite Street C1-D
Tooley Street L
Torrington Place F8-F9-G
Tottenham Court Road F9-F8-G8-G
Trafalgar Square G5-G
Tregunter Road A
Trevor Place C
Tufton Street G
Tudor Street I7-J
Trinity Street J4-K
Turks Row D1-D
Turnmill Street I9-I8-J
Tyers Street H
Ufford Street I4-J
Union Street J5-K
Upper Brook Street D
Upper Grosvenor Street D
Upper Ground I5-I6-J
Upper Thames Street J6-K6-L
Vauxhall Bridge G1-H
Vauxhall Bridge Road E3-F3-F2-G
Vauxhall Street H2-H1-I
Vauxhall Walk H
Vere Street E
Victoria Embankment H5-H6-I6-J
Victoria Road A3-A
Victoria Street E3-F3-F4-G
Vincent Square F2-F
Vincent Street F2-G
Walnut Tree Walk I
Walton Street C2-C
Walworth Road J3-K3-K2-K
Wardour Street F6-F
Warren Street E9-F
Warrington Crescent A8-A
Warwick Avenue A
Warwick Square F
Warwick Street F
Warwick Way E2-F
Waterloo Bridge H6-H5-I
Waterloo Road I5-I4-J
Watling Street K
Webber Street I4-J
Welbeck Street D8-D7-E
Wells Street F7-F
Westbourne Terrace A7-A6-B
Westcott Road J
Westminster Bridge H
Westminster Bridge Road H4-I4-J
Westmoreland Road K1-L
Westmoreland Terrace E
Weston Street F4-F
West Square J
Westway A7-A8-B
Wetherby Gardens A
Weymouth Street D8-E
Whitcomb Street G
Whitecross Street K8-K
Whitefriars Street I
Whitehall G4-G5-H
Whitehall Place G
Whiteheads Grove C
Whitfield Street F8-F
Wigmore Street D7-E
Wild Street H
Willow Place F2-F
Wilson Street L
Wilton Crescent D
Wilton Place D
Wilton Road E3-F3-F
Wimpole Street D8-E8-F
Winchester Street E2-E1-F
Wincott Street I
Woburn Place G
Wood Street K7-K
Woolers Street K2-L2-L1-K
Worship Street L
Yeomans Row C
York Gate D
York Road H4-H5-I
York Street C
York Terrace D8-D

London

History, tradition, culture, commerce, grandeur and beauty are just a few of the ingredients that make up England's magical capital. London's history begins in the 1st century when the Romans bridged the Thames in order to reach Colchester. An important city rapidly developed and right up until the 16th century London stayed more or less within the limits of the original Roman walls. However, from the 1600s onwards the city grew at an amazing rate, and even the Great Fire of 1666 – to which we owe the creation of the present St Paul's Cathedral and many other churches designed by Wren – did not halt expansion. The Thames winds through the heart of London and along its banks stand some of the city's most famous landmarks. Just by Westminster Bridge are the Houses of Parliament, easily distinguished by the clock-tower affectionately known the world over as Big Ben. Originally Westminster Palace, Charles Barry designed the present Gothic building, and much of its lavish decoration is the work of Augustus Pugin. Downstream, past the new complex of buildings including the Festival Hall and the National Theatre, is St Paul's Cathedral. Despite surrounding office blocks, the majesty of its enormous dome is not diminished. Next comes Tower Bridge and the Tower of London which, in its time, has been royal residence, prison, stronghold and place of execution.

However, London is not by any means all grand and famous buildings. Another of its many facets is its variety of shops. These range from the luxurious, prestigious Knightsbridge stores, led by Harrods, to the dozens of street markets, each with their own unique character. Covent Garden, Billingsgate, Smithfield and Petticoat Lane have become household names, but traders sell their wares throughout the city, and specialist shops steeped in tradition cater for individual tastes.

Yet another contrasting aspect of London is its parks and gardens. Best-known of these are the Royal parks. St James's, Green Park, Regent's Park – home of the London Zoo – and Hyde Park are all welcome havens from the busy streets. Past kings and queens were responsible for these green spaces and, in turn, their palaces add grace and splendour to the city. Buckingham Palace with its daily Changing of the Guard – just one of the ceremonies that flourish in London – takes pride of place, but St James's Palace and Kensington Palace deserve no less attention.

No account of London is complete without mentioning its superb theatres, concert halls, galleries and museums. As a cultural centre the capital plays host to the world's greatest performers and gives space to some of its greatest treasures.

Theatres, Concert Halls and Cinemas
A Guide to Entertainments in the Centre of London

THEATRES AND CONCERT HALLS

1 **Adelphi**, The Strand, WC2. Tel: 836 7611
2 **Albery**, St Martin's Lane, WC2. Tel: 836 3878
3 **Aldwych**, Aldwych, WC2. Tel: 836 6404
4 **Ambassadors**, West Street, WC2. Tel: 836 1171
5 **Apollo**, Shaftesbury Avenue, W1. Tel: 437 2663
6 **Apollo** (Victoria), Wilton Road, SW1. Tel: 828 8665 (Not on plan)
7 **Arts** (Theatre Club), Gt Newport Street, WC2. Tel: 836 3334
8 **Astoria**, Charing Cross Road, WC2. Tel: 734 4291
9 **Barbican Centre**, Silk Street, EC2. Tel: 628 8795 (Not on plan)
10 **Cambridge**, Earlham Street, WC2. Tel: 836 6056
11 **Coliseum**, St Martin's Lane, WC2. Tel: 836 3161
12 **Comedy**, Panton Street, SW1. Tel: 830 2578
13 **Criterion**, Piccadilly, W1. Tel: 9303216
14 **Drury Lane**, Theatre Royal, Catherine Street, WC2. Tel: 836 8108
15 **Duchess**, Catherine Street, WC2. Tel: 836 8243
16 **Duke of York's**, St Martin's Lane, WC2. Tel: 836 5122
17 **Fortune**, Russell Street, WC2. Tel: 836 2238
18 **Garrick**, Charing Cross Road, WC2. Tel: 836 4601
19 **Globe**, Shaftesbury Avenue, W1. Tel: 437 1592
20 **Haymarket**, Theatre Royal, Haymarket, W1. Tel: 930 9832
21 **Her Majesty's**, Haymarket, SW1. Tel: 930 6606
22 **Jeanetta Cochrane**, Theobalds Road, WC1. Tel: 242 7040.
23 **Lyric**, Shaftesbury Avenue, W1. Tel: 437 3686
24 **Mayfair**, Berkeley Street, W1. Tel: 629 3036

25 **Mermaid**, Puddle Dock, EC4. Tel: 236 5568 (Not on plan)
26 **National Theatre**, South Bank, SE1. Tel: 928 2252
27 **New London**, Parker Street, WC2. Tel: 405 0072
28 **Old Vic**, Waterloo Road, SE1. Tel: 928 7616
29 **Palace**, Shaftesbury Avenue, W1. Tel: 437 6834
30 **Palladium**, Argyll Street, W1. Tel: 437 7373.
31 **Phoenix**, Charing Cross Road, WC2. Tel: 836 2294
32 **Piccadilly**, Denman Street, W1. Tel: 437 4506
33 **Prince Edward**, Old Compton Street, W1. Tel: 930 6877
34 **Prince of Wales**, Coventry Street, W1. Tel: 930 8681
35 **Queen Elizabeth Hall**, South Bank, SE1. Tel: 928 3191
36 **Queen's**, Shaftesbury Avenue, W1. Tel: 734 1166
37 **Royal Court**, Sloane Square, SW1. Tel: 730 1745 (Not on plan)
38 **Royal Festival Hall**, South Bank, SE1. Tel: 928 3191
39 **Royal Opera House**, Covent Garden, WC2. Tel: 240 1066
40 **Royalty**, Portugal Street, WC2. Tel: 405 8004
41 **St Martin's**, West Street, WC2. Tel: 836 1443
42 **Sadler's Wells**, Roseberry Avenue, EC1. Tel: 278 8916 (Not on plan)
43 **Savoy**, Strand, WC2. Tel: 836 8888
44 **Shaftesbury**, Shaftesbury Avenue, WC2. Tel: 836 6596
45 **Strand**, Aldwych, WC2. Tel: 836 2660
46 **Vanburgh**, Malet Street, WC1. Tel: 580 7982 (Not on plan)
47 **Vaudeville**, Strand, WC2. Tel: 836 9988
48 **Victoria Palace**, Victoria Street, SW1. Tel: 834 1317 (Not on plan)

49 **Warehouse**, (Donmar), Earlham Street, WC2. Tel: 836 1071
50 **Westminster**, Palace Street, SW1. Tel: 834 0283 (Not on plan)
51 **Whitehall**, Whitehall, SW1. Tel: 930 7765
52 **Wigmore Hall**, Wigmore Street, W1. Tel: 935 2141
53 **Wyndhams**, Charing Cross Road, WC2. Tel: 836 3028.
54 **Young Vic**, The Cut, SE1. Tel: 928 6363

CINEMAS

1 **ABC 1 & 2**, Shaftesbury Avenue, WC2. Tel: 836 8861
2 **Acadamy 1, 2 & 3**, Oxford Street, W1. Tel: 437 2981
3 **Biograph**, Wilton Road, SW1. Tel: 834 1624 (Not on plan)
4 **Cinecenta**, Panton Street, W1. Tel: 930 0631
5 **Cinecenta**, Piccadilly, W1. Tel: 437 3561
6 **Classic**, Charing Cross Road, WC2. Tel: 930 6915
7 **Classic Complex**, Haymarket, SW1. Tel: 839 1527
8 **Classic, 1, 2, 3, 4 & 5**, Oxford Street, W1. Tel: 636 0310
9 **Classic**, Shaftesbury Avenue, W1. Tel: 734 5414
10 **Classic Complex**, Tottenham Court Road, W1. Tel: 636 6148
11 **Curzon**, Curzon Street, W1. Tel: 499 3737
12 **Dominion**, Tottenham Court Road, W1. Tel: 580 9562
13 **Empire**, Leicester Square, WC2. Tel: 437 1234.
14 **Eros**, Piccadilly Circus, W1. Tel: 437 3839
15 **Filmcenta**, Charing Cross Road, WC2. Tel: 437 4815
16 **Gate 2**, Brunswick Square, WC1. Tel: 837 8402 (Not on plan)
17 **Gate, Mayfair**, Mayfair Hotel, Stratton Street, W1. Tel: 493 2031

18 **Institution of Contemporary Arts**, Carlton House Terrace SW1. Tel: 930 6393
19 **Leicester Square Theatre**, Leicester Square, WC2. Tel: 930 5252
20 **Lumiere**, St Martin's Lane, WC2. Tel: 836 0691
21 **Minema**, Knightsbridge, SW1. Tel: 235 6225
22 **Moulin Cinema Complex**, Gt Windmill Street, W1. Tel: 437 1653
23 **National Film Theatre**, South Bank, SE1. Tel: 928 3232
24 **Odeon**, Haymarket, SW1. Tel: 930 2738
25 **Odeon**, Leicester Square, WC2. Tel: 930 6111
26 **Odeon**, Marble Arch, W2. Tel: 723 2011 (Not on plan)
27 **Plaza, 1, 2, 3 & 4**, Regent Street, W1. Tel: 437 1234
28 **Prince Charles**, Leicester Place, WC2. Tel: 437 8181
29 **Scene, 1, 2, 3 & 4**, Swiss Centre, Leicester Square, WC2. Tel: 439 4470
30 **Sherlock Holmes Centa**, Baker Street, W1. Tel: 935 2772
31 **Studio 1, 2, 3 & 4**, Oxford Street, W1. Tel: 437 3300.
32 **Times Centa 1 & 2**, Chiltern Court, Baker Street, NW1. Tel: 935 9772
33 **Warner West End, 1, 2, 3 & 4**, Cranbourn Street, WC2. Tel: 439 0791

Key

Parking — P
One Way Street — ➜
Cinema — ●
Theatre — ●
Underground — ⊖

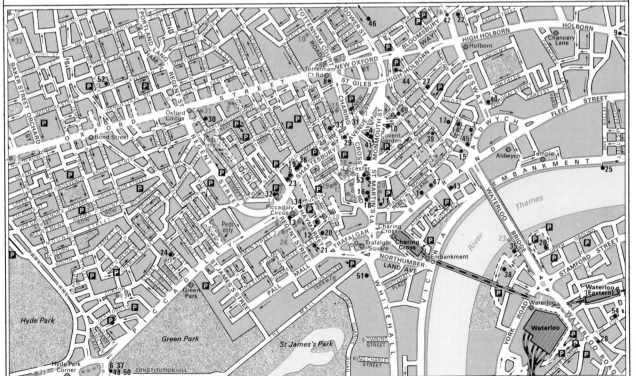

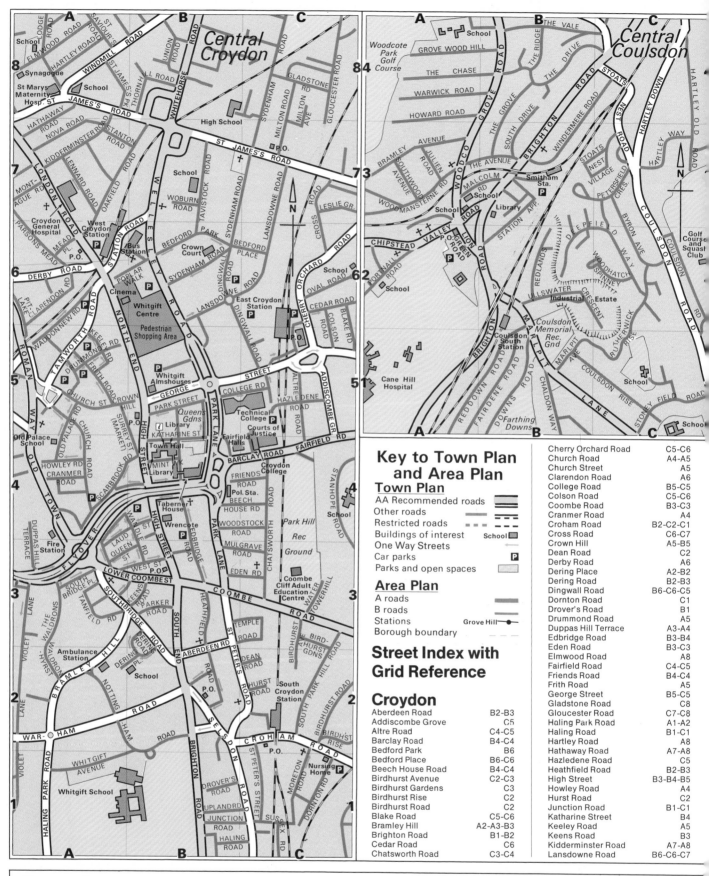

Key to Town Plan and Area Plan

Town Plan

AA Recommended roads	
Other roads	
Restricted roads	
Buildings of interest	School
One Way Streets	←
Car parks	P
Parks and open spaces	

Area Plan

A roads	
B roads	
Stations	Grove Hill ●—
Borough boundary	

Street Index with Grid Reference

Croydon

Aberdeen Road	B2-B3
Addiscombe Grove	C5
Altre Road	C4-C5
Barclay Road	B4-C4
Bedford Park	B6
Bedford Place	B6-C6
Beech House Road	B4-C4
Birdhurst Avenue	C2-C3
Birdhurst Gardens	C3
Birdhurst Rise	C2
Birdhurst Road	C2
Blake Road	C5-C6
Bramley Hill	A2-A3-B3
Brighton Road	B1-B2
Cedar Road	C6
Chatsworth Road	C3-C4
Cherry Orchard Road	C5-C6
Church Road	A4-A5
Church Street	A5
Clarendon Road	A6
College Road	B5-C5
Colson Road	C5-C6
Coombe Road	B3-C3
Cranmer Road	A4
Croham Road	B2-C2-C1
Cross Road	C6-C7
Crown Hill	A5-B5
Dean Road	C2
Derby Road	A6
Dering Place	A2-B2
Dering Road	B2-B3
Dingwall Road	B6-C6-C5
Dornton Road	C1
Drover's Road	B1
Drummond Road	A5
Duppas Hill Terrace	A3-A4
Edbridge Road	B3-B4
Eden Road	B3-C3
Elmwood Road	A8
Fairfield Road	C4-C5
Friends Road	B4-C4
Frith Road	A5
George Street	B5-C5
Gladstone Road	C8
Gloucester Road	C7-C8
Haling Park Road	A1-A2
Haling Road	B1-C1
Hartley Road	A8
Hathaway Road	A7-A8
Hazledene Road	C5
Heathfield Road	B2-B3
High Street	B3-B4-B5
Howley Road	A4
Hurst Road	C2
Junction Road	B1-C1
Katharine Street	B4
Keeley Road	A5
Keens Road	B3
Kidderminster Road	A7-A8
Lansdowne Road	B6-C6-C7

Croydon

Lofty office blocks piercing the south London skyline, one of the largest shopping centres in south-east England and modern developments like the Whitgift Centre and Fairfields Hall (an arts and exhibitions complex containing the Ashcroft Theatre) characterise modern Croydon — but it still has numerous features recalling its prosperity in earlier times. The Archbishops'

Palace (now a girls' school) was occupied by the Archbishops of Canterbury until the 18th century. The oldest shop in the town can be seen in South End, a 16th- to 17th-century building with an overhanging upper storey. Wrencote, in the High Street, is a fine example of an 18th-century town house. Other places of interest include the 16th-century Whitgift Hospital (an almshouse) the Flemish style 19th-century Town Hall, and the Parish Church of St John the Baptist, rebuilt in

1867 — after a fire — by Sir Gilbert Scott, in the original 15th-century style.

Purley grew rapidly after the end of the 18th century. There are good shopping facilities and the Village Green on the Webb Estate has been designated a conservation area.

Coulsdon Beautiful Farthing Downs and Happy Valley (where nature trails can be followed) lie close by. The Church of St John the Evangelist is a fine example of 13th-century architecture.

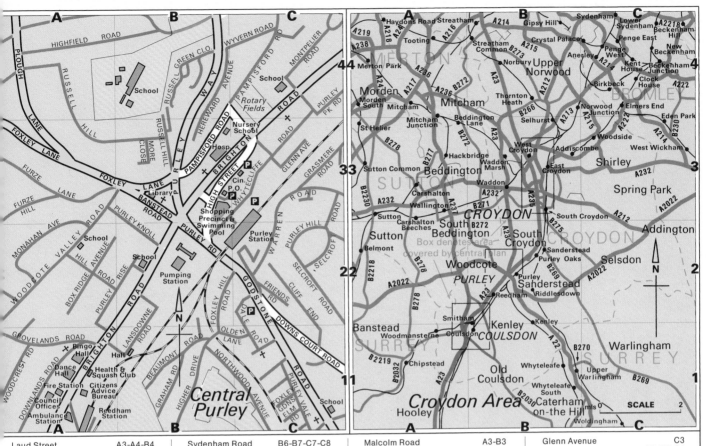

Central Purley / **Croydon Area**

Laud Street	A3-A4-B4	Sydenham Road	B6-B7-C7-C8
Lennard Road	A7	Tamworth Road	A5-A6
Leslie Grove	C7	Tanfield Road	A3
Lodge Road	A8	Tavistock Road	B6-B7
London Road	A6-A7	Temple Road	B3-C3-B3
Lower Coombe Street	A3-B3	The Waldrons	A3
Mead Place	A6	Thornhill Road	B8
Milton Avenue	C7-C8	Union Road	B8
Milton Road	C7-C8	Upland Road	B1-C1
Mint Walk	B4	Violet Lane	A1-A2-A3
Montague Road	A7	Waddon New Road	A5-A6
Moreton Road	C1-C2	Waldronhyst	A2
Mulgrave Road	B3-C3	Wandle Road	A4-B4-B3
North End	A6-A5-B5	Warham Road	A2-B2
Nottingham Road	A2-B2	Water Tower Hill	C3
Nova Road	A7	Wellesley Road	B5-B6-B7
Oakfield Road	A6-A7-B7	West Street	A3-B3
Old Palace Road	A4-A5	Windmill Road	A8-B8
Old Town	A3-A4	Whitehorse Road	B7-B8
Oval Road	C6	Whitgift Avenue	A1-B1-B2
Park Lane	B3-B4-B5	Woburn Road	B7
Park Street	B5	Woodstock Road	B4-C4
Parker Road	B3		
Parsons Mead	A6-A7		
Pitlake	A6		
Poplar Walk	A6-B6		
Queen Street	A3-B3		
Roman Way	A5-A6		
St James's Park	A8		
St James's Walk	A7-A8-B8-B7-C7		
St Peter's Road	B3-B2-C2-B2		
St Peter's Street	C1-C2		
St Saviour's Road	A8		
Selsdon Road	B2-B1-C1		
Scarbrook Road	A4-B4		
South Bridge Place	A3		
South Bridge Road	A3-B3-B2		
South End	B2-B3		
South Park Hill Road	C2-C3		
Stanhope Road	C3-C4		
Stanton Road	A7-B7		
Station Road	A6-B6-B7		
Surrey Street	A5-B5-B4		
Sussex Road	C1		

Coulsdon

Bramley Avenue	A3
Brighton Road	A1-B1-B2-A2-A3-B3-B4-C4
Byron Avenue	C2-C3
Chaldon Way	B1
Chipstead Valley Road	A2-A3-B3
Coulsdon Court Road	C1-C2
Coulsdon Rise	B1-C1
Coulsdon Road	C1-C2-C3
Deepfield Way	B2-C2
Downs Road	B1
Fairdene Road	A1-B1
Grove Wood Hill	A4-B4
Hartley Down	C3-C4
Hartley Old Road	C3-C4
Hartley Way	C3
Howard Road	A3-A4
Julien Road	A3
Lion Green Road	A2

Malcolm Road	A3-B3	Glenn Avenue	C3
Marlpit Avenue	B1	Godstone Road	B2-C2-C1
Marlpit Lane	B2-B1-C1	Graham Road	B1
Petersfield Crescent	B3-C3	Grasmere Road	C3
Portnall Road	A2	Grovelands Road	A1
Reddown Road	A1-B1-B2	Hereward Avenue	B3-B4
Redlands	B2	High Street	B2-B3-C3
Rutherwick Rise	C1-C2	Higher Drive	B1
South Drive	B3-B4	Highfield Road	A4-B4
Southwood Avenue	A3	Hill Road	A2
Station Approach	B2-B3	Lansdowne Road	A1-B1-B2
Stoats Nest Road	C3-C4	Monahan Avenue	A2-A3-A2
Stoats Nest Village	B3-C3	Montpelier Road	C4
Stoney Field Road	C1	More Close	B3
The Avenue	A3-B3	Northwood Avenue	B1-C1
The Chase	A4-B4	Olden Lane	B1-C1
The Drive	B4-C4	Pampisford Road	B3-B4-C4
The Grove	B3-B4	Plough Lane	A3-A4
The Ridge	B4	Purley Hill	C2
The Vale	B4-C4	Purley Knoll	A3-B3-B2
Ullswater Crescent	B2-C2	Purley Park Road	C4
Warwick Road	A4-B4	Purley Rise	A1-A2-B2
Windermere Road	B3-B4-C4	Purley Road	B2
Woodcote Grove Road	A3-A4-B4	Purley Vale	C1
Woodhatch Spinney	B2-C2	Purley Way	B3-B4
Woodmansterne Road	A3	Russell Green Close	B4
		Russell Hill	A4-A3-B3-B4
		Selcroft Road	C2-C3

Purley

Banstead Road	B3	Warren Road	C2-C3
Beaumont Road	B1	Whytecliffe Road	B2-B3-C3-C4
Box Ridge Avenue	A2	Woodcote Valley Road	A2-A3-B3
Brighton Road	A1-A2-B2-B3-C3-C4	Woodcrest Road	A1
Cliff End	C1-C2	Wyvern Road	B4-C4
Dale Road	C1-C2		
Downlands Road	A1		
Downs Court Road	C1-C2		
Elm Road	C1		
Foxley Gardens	C1		
Foxley Hill Road	B1-B2-C2		
Foxley Lane	A3-B3		
Friends Road	C2		
Furze Hill	A3		
Furze Lane	A3		

CROYDON
Beyond the gleaming blue glass of St Crispins House, the extensive Fairfield Halls complex offers concerts for music-lovers, with drama at the Ashcroft Theatre and exhibitions at the Arnhem Gallery.

Ealing

The Ealing Comedies, cinema classics of the 1940s and 1950s were made in studios overlooking Ealing Green — studios which have now been taken over by the BBC for the production of television films. Ealing is a pleasantly leafy London suburb. Fine shopping facilities can be found in the Broadway area and buildings of interest include the fine Victorian Town Hall, and the former Pitshanger Manor, in Walpole Park, which has become the central library.

Southall has been known for its cattle market since the late 17th century, and this still takes place every Wednesday, close to the High Street. In recent years the Southall area has become the home of numerous Commonwealth immigrants, and it now has a distinctive Asian character of its own, particularly in the main Broadway shopping area. Southall Manor, standing on the Green, dates originally from the 16th century.

Hammersmith is seen by most of those who pass through as a vista of roof tops — the view from the flyover built to ease congestion where traffic from the Great West Road and Hammersmith Bridge meet with the many vehicles entering and leaving Central London. Hammersmith is also the site of the Lyric Theatre, known for its pre-West End productions; the BBC TV Studios lie a short distance to the north.

14

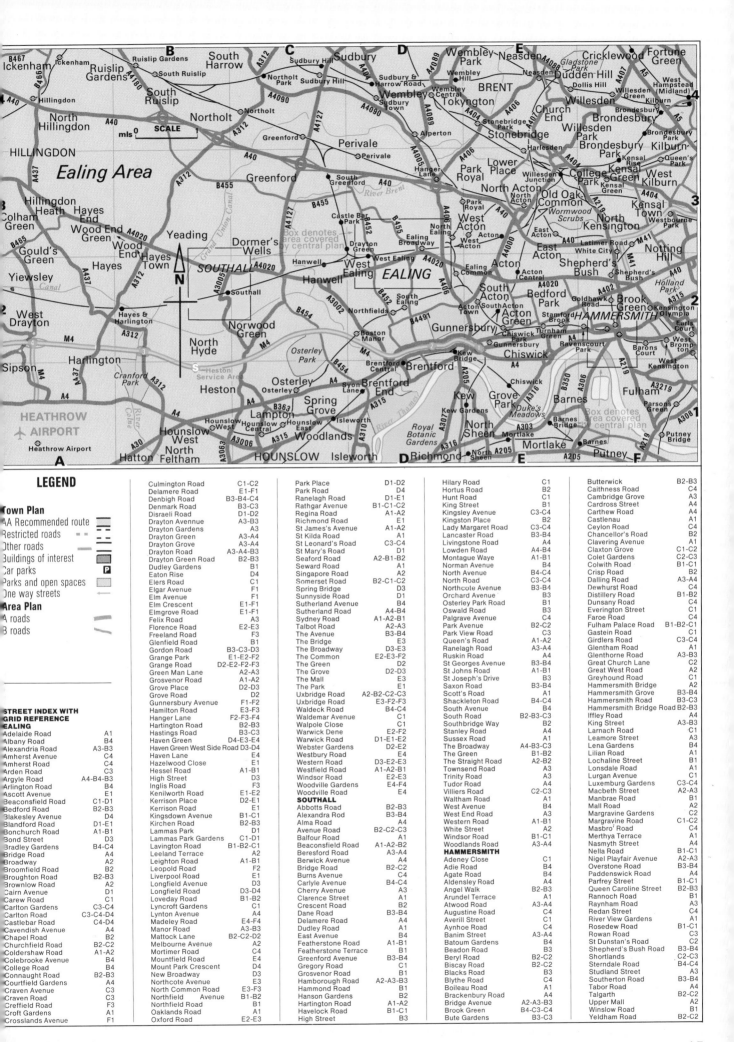

LEGEND

Town Plan

- AA Recommended route
- Restricted roads
- Other roads
- Buildings of interest
- Car parks
- Parks and open spaces
- One way streets

Area Plan

- A roads
- B roads

STREET INDEX WITH GRID REFERENCE

EALING

Adelaide Road	A1
Albany Road	B4
Alexandria Road	A3-B3
Amherst Avenue	C4
Amherst Road	C4
Arden Road	C3
Argyle Road	A4-B4-B3
Arlington Road	B4
Ascott Avenue	E1
Beaconsfield Road	C1-D1
Bedford Road	B2-B3
Blakesley Avenue	D4
Blandford Road	D1-E1
Bonchurch Road	A1-B1
Bond Street	D3
Bradley Gardens	B4-C4
Bridge Road	A4
Broadway	A2
Broomfield Road	B2
Broughton Road	B2-B3
Brownlow Road	A2
Cairn Avenue	D1
Carew Road	C1
Carlton Gardens	C3-C4
Carlton Road	C3-C4-D4
Castlebar Road	C4-D4
Cavendish Avenue	A4
Chapel Road	B2
Churchfield Road	B2-C2
Coldershaw Road	A1-A2
Colebrooke Avenue	B4
College Road	B4
Connaught Road	B2-B3
Courtfield Gardens	A4
Craven Avenue	C3
Craven Road	C3
Creffield Road	F3
Croft Gardens	A1
Crosslands Avenue	F1
Culmington Road	C1-C2
Delamere Road	E1-F1
Denbigh Road	B3-B4-C4
Denmark Road	B3-C3
Disraeli Road	D1-D2
Drayton Avennue	A3-B3
Drayton Gardens	A3
Drayton Green	A3-A4
Drayton Grove	A3-A4
Drayton Road	A3-A4-B3
Drayton Green Road	B2-B3
Dudley Gardens	B1
Eaton Rise	D4
Elers Road	C1
Elgar Avenue	F1
Elm Avenue	F1
Elm Crescent	E1-F1
Elmgrove Road	E1-F1
Felix Road	A3
Florence Road	E2-E3
Freeland Road	F3
Glenfield Road	B1
Gordon Road	B3-C3-D3
Grange Park	E1-E2-F2
Grange Road	D2-E2-F2-F3
Green Man Lane	A2-A3
Grosvenor Road	A1-A2
Grove Place	D2-D3
Grove Road	D2
Gunnersbury Avenue	F1-F2
Hamilton Road	E3-F3
Hanger Lane	F2-F3-F4
Hartington Road	B2-B3
Hastings Road	B3-C3
Haven Green	D4-E3-E4
Haven Green West Side Road	D3-D4
Haven Lane	E4
Hazelwood Close	E1
Hessel Road	A1-B1
High Street	D3
Inglis Road	F3
Kenilworth Road	E1-E2
Kerrison Place	D2-E1
Kerrison Road	D2-E1
Kingsdown Avenue	B1-C1
Kirchen Road	B2-B3
Lammas Park	D1
Lammas Park Gardens	C1-D1
Lavington Road	B1-B2-C1
Leeland Terrace	A2
Leighton Road	A1-B1
Leopold Road	F2
Liverpool Road	E1
Longfield Avenue	D3
Longfield Road	D3-D4
Loveday Road	B1-B2
Lyncroft Gardens	C1
Lynton Avenue	A4
Madeley Road	E4-F4
Manor Road	A3-B3
Mattock Lane	B2-C2-D2
Melbourne Avenue	A2
Mortimer Road	C4
Mountfield Road	E4
Mount Park Crescent	D4
New Broadway	D3
Northcote Avenue	E3
North Common Road	E3-F3
Northfield Avenue	B1-B2
Northfield Road	B1
Oaklands Road	A1
Oxford Road	E2-E3

Park Place	D1-D2
Park Road	D4
Ranelagh Road	D1-E1
Rathgar Avenue	B1-C1-C2
Regina Road	A1-A2
Richmond Road	E1
St James's Avenue	A1-A2
St Kilda Road	A1
St Leonard's Road	C3-C4
St Mary's Road	D1
Seaford Road	A2-B1-B2
Seward Road	A1
Singapore Road	A2
Somerset Road	B2-C1-C2
Spring Bridge	D3
Sunnyside Road	D1
Sutherland Avenue	B4
Sutherland Road	A4-B4
Sydney Road	A1-A2-B1
Talbot Road	A2-A3
The Avenue	B3-B4
The Bridge	E3
The Broadway	D3-E3
The Common	E2-E3-F2
The Green	D2
The Grove	D2-D3
The Mall	E1
The Park	E1
Uxbridge Road	A2-B2-C2-C3
Uxbridge Road	E3-F2-F3
Waldeck Road	B4-C4
Waldemar Avenue	C1
Walpole Close	C1
Warwick Dene	E2-F2
Warwick Road	D1-E1-E2
Webster Gardens	D2-E2
Westbury Road	E4
Western Road	D3-E2-E3
Westfield Road	A1-A2-B1
Windsor Road	E2-E3
Woodville Gardens	E4-F4
Woodville Road	E4

SOUTHALL

Abbotts Road	B2-B3
Alexandra Rod	B3-B4
Alma Road	A4
Avenue Road	B2-C2-C3
Balfour Road	A4
Beaconsfield Road	A1-A2-B2
Beresford Road	A3-A4
Berwick Avenue	A4
Bridge Road	B2-C2
Burns Avenue	C4
Carlyle Avenue	B4-C4
Cherry Avenue	A3
Clarence Street	A1
Crescent Road	B2
Dane Road	B3-B4
Delamere Road	A4
Dudley Road	A1
East Avenue	A1-B1
Featherstone Road	A1-B1
Featherstone Terrace	B1
Greenford Avenue	B3-B4
Gregory Road	C1
Grosvenor Road	B1
Hamborough Road	A2-A3-B3
Hammond Road	B1
Hanson Gardens	B2
Hartington Road	A1-A2
Havelock Road	B1-C1
High Street	B3

Hilary Road	C1
Hortus Road	B2
Hunt Road	C1
King Street	B1
Kingsley Avenue	C3-C4
Kingston Place	B2
Lady Margaret Road	C3-C4
Lancaster Road	B3-B4
Livingstone Road	A4
Lowden Road	A4-B4
Montague Waye	A1-B1
Norman Avenue	B4
North Avenue	B4-C4
North Road	C3-C4
Northcote Avenue	B3-B4
Orchard Avenue	B3
Osterley Park Road	B1
Oswald Road	B3
Palgrave Avenue	C4
Park Avenue	B2-C2
Park View Road	C3
Queen's Road	A1-A2
Ranelagh Road	A3-A4
Ruskin Road	A4
St Georges Avenue	B3-B4
St Johns Road	A1-B1
St Joseph's Drive	B3
Saxon Road	B3-B4
Scott's Road	A1
Shackleton Road	B4-C4
South Avenue	C4
South Road	B2-B3-C3
Southbridge Way	B2
Stanley Road	A4
Sussex Road	A1
The Broadway	A4-B3-C3
The Green	B1-B2
The Straight Road	A2-B2
Townsend Road	A3
Trinity Road	A3
Tudor Road	A4
Villiers Road	C2-C3
Waltham Road	A1
West Avenue	B4
West End Road	A3
Western Road	A1-B1
White Street	A2
Windsor Road	B1-C1
Woodlands Road	A3-A4

HAMMERSMITH

Adeney Close	C1
Adie Road	B4
Agate Road	B4
Aldensley Road	A4
Angel Walk	B2-B3
Arundel Terrace	A1
Atwood Road	A3-A4
Augustine Road	C4
Averill Street	C1
Aynhoe Road	C4
Banim Street	A3-A4
Batoum Gardens	B4
Beadon Road	B3
Beryl Road	B2-C2
Biscay Road	B2-C2
Blacks Road	B3
Blythe Road	C4
Boileau Road	A1
Brackenbury Road	A4
Bridge Avenue	A2-A3-B3
Brook Green	B4-C3-C4
Bute Gardens	B3-C3

Butterwick	B2-B3
Caithness Road	C4
Cambridge Grove	A3
Cardross Street	A4
Carthew Road	A4
Castlenau	A1
Ceylon Road	C4
Chancellor's Road	B2
Clavering Avenue	A1
Claxton Grove	C1-C2
Colet Gardens	C2-C3
Colwith Road	B1-C1
Crisp Road	B2
Dalling Road	A3-A4
Dewhurst Road	C4
Distillery Road	B1-B2
Dunsany Road	C4
Everington Street	C1
Faroe Road	C4
Fulham Palace Road	B1-B2-C1
Gastein Road	C1
Girdlers Road	C3-C4
Glentham Road	A1
Glenthorne Road	A3-B3
Great Church Lane	C2
Great West Road	A2
Greyhound Road	C1
Hammersmith Bridge	A2
Hammersmith Grove	B3-B4
Hammersmith Road	B3-C3
Hammersmith Bridge Road	B2-B3
Iffley Road	A4
King Street	A3-B3
Larnach Road	C1
Leamore Street	A3
Lena Gardens	B4
Lilian Road	A1
Lochaline Street	B1
Lonsdale Road	A1
Lurgan Avenue	C1
Luxemburg Gardens	C3-C4
Macbeth Street	A2-A3
Manbrae Road	B1
Mall Road	A2
Margravine Gardens	C2
Margravine Road	C1-C2
Masbro' Road	C4
Merthya Terrace	A1
Nasmyth Street	A4
Nella Road	B1-C1
Nigel Playfair Avenue	A2-A3
Overstone Road	B3-B4
Paddenswick Road	A4
Parfrey Street	B1-C1
Queen Caroline Street	B2-B3
Rannoch Road	B1
Raynham Road	A3
Redan Street	C4
River View Gardens	A1
Rosedew Road	B1-C1
Rowan Road	C3
St Dunstan's Road	C2
Shepherd's Bush Road	B3-B4
Shortlands	C2-C3
Sterndale Road	B4-C4
Studland Street	A3
Southerton Road	B3-B4
Tabor Road	A4
Talgarth	B2-C2
Upper Mall	A2
Winslow Road	B1
Yeldham Road	B2-C2

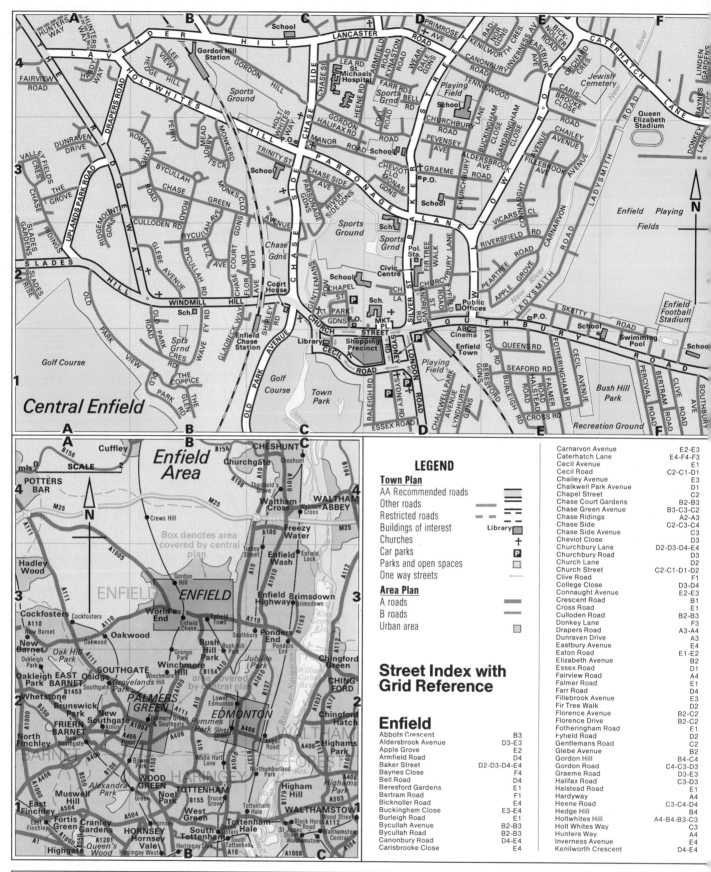

Central Enfield

Enfield Area

LEGEND

Town Plan

AA Recommended roads	
Other roads	
Restricted roads	
Buildings of interest	Library
Churches	✝
Car parks	P
Parks and open spaces	
One way streets	←

Area Plan

A roads	
B roads	
Urban area	

Street Index with Grid Reference

Enfield

Abbots Crescent	B3
Aldersbrook Avenue	D3-E3
Apple Grove	E2
Armfield Road	D4
Baker Street	D2-D3-D4-E4
Baynes Close	F4
Bell Road	D4
Beresford Gardens	E1
Bertram Road	F1
Bicknoller Road	E4
Buckingham Close	E3-E4
Burleigh Road	E1
Bycullah Avenue	B2-B3
Bycullah Road	B2-B3
Canonbury Road	D4-E4
Carisbrooke Close	E4
Carnarvon Avenue	E2-E3
Caterhatch Lane	E4-F4-F3
Cecil Avenue	E1
Cecil Road	C2-C1-D1
Chailey Avenue	E3
Chalkwell Park Avenue	D1
Chapel Street	C2
Chase Court Gardens	B2-B3
Chase Green Avenue	B3-C3-C2
Chase Ridings	A2-A3
Chase Side	C2-C3-C4
Chase Side Avenue	C3
Cheviot Close	D3
Churchbury Lane	D2-D3-D4-E4
Churchbury Road	D3
Church Lane	D2
Church Street	C2-C1-D1-D2
Clive Road	F1
College Close	D3-D4
Connaught Avenue	E2-E3
Crescent Road	B1
Cross Road	E1
Culloden Road	B2-B3
Donkey Lane	F3
Drapers Road	A3-A4
Dunraven Drive	A3
Eastbury Avenue	E4
Eaton Road	E1-E2
Elizabeth Avenue	B2
Essex Road	D1
Fairview Road	A4
Falmer Road	E1
Farr Road	D4
Fillebrook Avenue	E3
Fir Tree Walk	D2
Florence Avenue	B2-C2
Florence Drive	B2-C2
Fotheringham Road	E1
Fyfield Road	D2
Gentlemans Road	C2
Glebe Avenue	B2
Gordon Hill	B4-C4
Gordon Road	C4-C3-D3
Graeme Road	D3-E3
Halifax Road	C3-D3
Halstead Road	E1
Hardyway	A4
Heene Road	C3-C4-D4
Hedge Hill	B4
Holtwhites Hill	A4-B4-B3-C3
Holt Whites Way	C3
Hunters Way	A4
Inverness Avenue	E4
Kenilworth Crescent	D4-E4

Enfield

Built in the 17th century to bring fresh water from Hertford to London, the attractive New River waterway still winds through the centre of Enfield, separating the Town Park from the Golf Course. Although this residential town on the edge of the Green Belt saw a good deal of expansion when the railways arrived in the 19th century, much of the older part has survived.

Near the 12th- to 14th-century parish church are Holly Walk and Gentleman's Row, which has a number of picturesque old cottages, including one where 19th-century essayist Charles Lamb would often stay with his sister Mary. They later rented a house close by in Chase Side.

Forty Hall, at nearby Forty Hill, dates from the 17th century and has a local history museum.

Edmonton's parish church has some Norman features, and Charles Lamb is buried in the churchyard. Edmonton itself is a residential area with modern shopping facilities centred around the open air market and pedestrian precinct at Edmonton Green.

Palmers Green became a fashionable residential suburb during the early part of the present century, and is the home of the Intimate Theatre, which stages many pre-West End productions. The attractive Broomfield Park (being restored) contains a museum of local history.

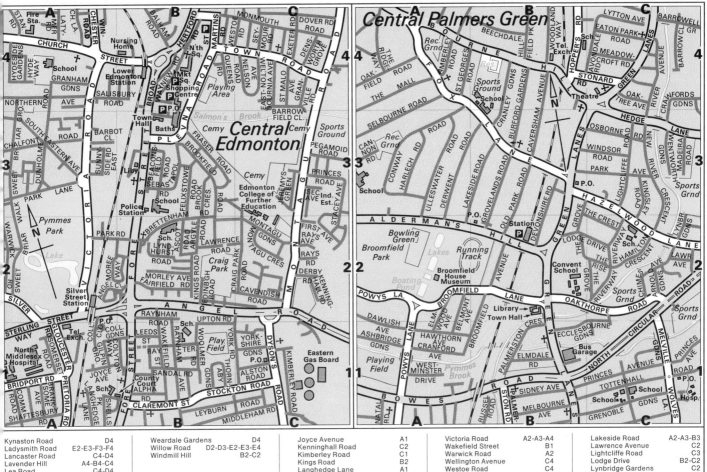

Central Edmonton map (grid A-D, 1-4)

Central Palmers Green map (grid A-C, 1-4)

Kynaston Road	D4
Ladysmith Road	E2-E3-F3-F4
Lancaster Road	C4-D4
Lavender Hill	A4-B4-C4
Lea Road	C4-D4
Lee View	B4
Linden Gardens	F4
Little Park Gardens	C2
London Road	D1
Lyndhurst Gardens	D1
Manor Road	C3-D3
Monastry Gardens	D3
Monks Close	B3-C3
Monks Road	B3
Old Park Avenue	B1-C1-C2
Old Park Road	B1-B2
Old Park View	A2-A1-B1
Orchard Crescent	E4
Parsonage Gardens	C2-C3
Parsonage Lane	C3-D3-D2
Peartree Road	D2-E2
Percival Road	F1
Perry Mead	B3-B4
Pevensey Avenue	D3
Primrose Avenue	D4
Queens Road	E1
Radnor Gardens	E4
Raleigh Road	D1
Ridgemount Gardens	A2-A3
Riversfield Road	D2-E2
Riverside Gardens	C3
Rowantree Road	A3-B3
St Andrews Road	D2
Sandringham Close	D3
Seaford Road	E1
Shirley Road	C1-C2
Silver Street	
Sketty Road	E2-F2-F1
Slades Gardens	A2-A3
Slades Hill	A2-B2
Slades Rise	A2
Southbury Avenue	F1
Southbury Road	D1-D2-E2-E1-F1
Sydney Road	D1
The Coppice	B1
The Glen	B1
The Grove	A3
The Ridgeway	A4-A3-A2-B2
Tenniswood Road	D4-E4-E3
Trinity Street	C3
Uplands Park Road	A2-A3
Valley Fields Crescent	A3
Vicars Close	E2-E3
Waverley Road	B1-B2

Weardale Gardens	D4
Willow Road	D2-D3-E2-E3-E4
Windmill Hill	B2-C2

Edmonton

Alpha Road	B1
Alston Road	C1
Angel Close	A2-B2
Angel Road	B2-C2-C1
Argyle Road	B2
Ascot Road	B2
Balham Road	B4
Barbot Close	A3
Barrowfield Close	C3-C4
Beconsfield Road	B3
Branksome Avenue	A1
Brettenham Road	B2
Bridport Road	A1
Broadway	B4
Brook Crescent	B3
Brookfield Road	B3
Cavendish Road	C2
Chalfont Road	A3
Church Lane	
Church Street	A4-B4
Claremont Street	B1
College Close	A1-A2
College Gardens	A1-B1
Colyton Way	B1
Commercial Road	A1
Craig Park Road	C2
Densworth Grove	C4
Derby Road	C2
Dover Road	C4
Dunholme Road	A3-A4
Dyson's Road	C1-C2
Eastbournia Avenue	C4
Edinburgh Road	B2
Exeter Road	C4
Fairfield Road	B2
Felixstowe Road	B3
First Avenue	C2
Fore Street	A1-B1-B2-B3-B4
Fraser Road	B3
Gilpin Grove	A1
Gloucester Road	A1
Granham Gardens	A4
Granville Road	C4
Hertford Road	B4
Hydeside Gardens	A4
Hyde Way	A4
Jeremys Green	C3

Joyce Avenue	A1
Kenninghall Road	C2
Kimberley Road	C1
Kings Road	B2
Langhedge Lane	A1
Latymer Road	A4
Lawrence Road	B2-C2
Leeds Street	B1
Leyburn Road	B1-C1
Lyndhurst Road	B2
Middleham Road	B1-C1
Monmouth Road	B4-C4
Montagu Crescent	C2
Montagu Gardens	C2
Montagu Road	C2-C3-C4
Moree Way	A2-B2
Morley Avenue	B2
Nelson Road	C4
New Road	B4
Northern Avenue	A4
Park Lane	A3
Park Road	A2-B2
Pegamoid Road	C3
Plevena Road	B3-B4
Pretoria Road	A1
Princes Road	C3
Queens Road	B4
Raynham Avenue	B1-B2
Raynham Road	B2
Raynham Terrace	B1
Rays Avenue	C2
Rays Road	C2
St Malo Avenue	C4
St Martins Road	B4
Sebastapol Road	B3
Salisbury Road	A4-B4
Sandal Road	B1
Second Avenue	C3
Seymour Road	C4
Shaftesbury Road	A1
Silver Street	A1-B1
Snells Park	A1-B1
Somerset Road	A1
South Eastern Avenue	A3
Stacey Avenue	C2-C3
Stanley Road	A4
Sterling Way	A1-A2
Stockton Road	B1-C1
Sunnyside Road East	A3
Sweet Briar Grove	A3-A4
Sweet Briar Walk	A2-A3
Thornaby Gardens	B1
Town Road	B4-C4
Upton Road	B1

Victoria Road	A2-A3-A4
Wakefield Street	B1
Warwick Road	A2
Wellington Avenue	C4
Westoe Road	C4
Winchester Road	A4
Woolmer Road	B1
York Road	B1-B2-C1-C2
Yorkshire Gardens	C1

Palmers Green

Alderman's Hill	A2-B2
Amberley Road	A4
Arnold Gardens	C2
Ashbridge Gardens	A1
Avondale Road	B4-C4
Barrow Close	C4
Barrowell Grove	C4
Beechdale	B4
Belmont Avenue	A1-A2
Bourne Hill	A4-B4
Bowes Road	A1-B1
Broomfield Avenue	A1-B1-B2
Broomfield Lane	A2-B2
Burford Gardens	B3-B4
Cambridge Terrace	C1-C2
Cannon Road	A3
Caversham Avenue	B3-B4
Chimes Avenue	C2
Conway Road	A3-A4
Cranford Avenue	A1
Cranley Gardens	B3-B4
Crawfords Gardens	C3-C4
Dawlish Avenue	A1-A2
Derwent Road	A2-A3-B3
Devonshire Road	B2-B3
Eaton Park Road	C4
Ecclesbourne Gardens	B1-C1
Elmdale Road	B1
Elmwood Avenue	A1-A2
Fox Lane	A4-B4-B3
Green Lanes	B1-B2-B3-C3-C4
Grenoble Gardens	B1-C1
Grovelands Road	B2-B3
Hamilton Crescent	C2
Harlech Road	A3
Hawthorn Avenue	A1
Hazelwood Lane	B3-C3-C2
Hedge Lane	C4-C3
Hillfield Park	B4
Hopper's Road	B4
Kingsley Road	C2-C3

Lakeside Road	A2-A3-B3
Lawrence Avenue	C2
Lightcliffe Road	C3
Lodge Drive	B2-C2
Lynbridge Gardens	C2
Lytton Avenue	C4
Madeira Road	C3
Meadowcroft Road	C4
Melbourne Avenue	B1
Melville Gardens	C1-C2
Natal Road	A1
New River Crescent	C2-C3
North Circular Road	B1-C1-C2
Oakfield Road	A4
Oakthorpe Road	B2-C2
Oaktree Avenue	C4
Old Park Road	B2-B3
Osbourne Road	C3
Palmerston Crescent	B1
Palmerston Road	B1
Park Avenue	B3-C3
Powys Lane	A2
Princes Avenue	B1-C1
River Avenue	C3-C4
Riverway	C2
Russel Road	B1
St George's Road	A4-B4
Selbourne Road	A3-A4
Sidney Avenue	B1
Stonard Road	B4-C4
The Crest	B2-C2
The Grove	B3-B2-BC
The Mall	A4
The Ridgeway	A4
The Rise	C2
Tottenhall Road	B1-C1
Ulleswater Road	A2-A3
Wentworth Gardens	C3
Westminster Drive	A1
Windsor Road	B3-C3
Wolves Lane	C1
Woodland Way	B4

ENFIELD
Lamb's Cottage in Gentleman's Row — Charles Lamb and his sister Mary came to Enfield to stay with friends in 1825 and liked it so much that they made repeated visits back and eventually decided to settle here.

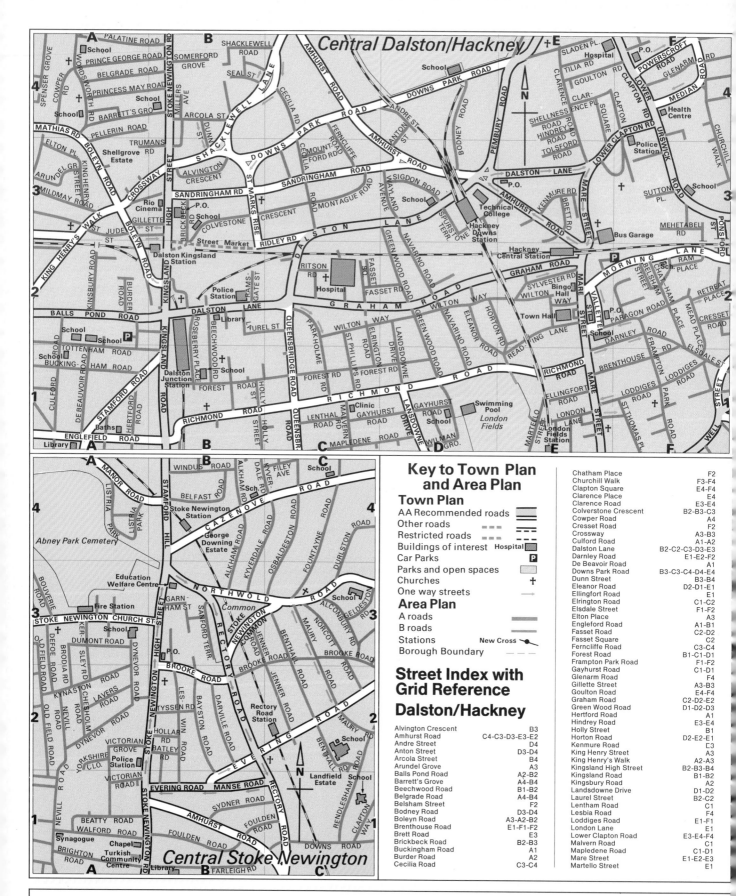

Key to Town Plan and Area Plan

Town Plan

AA Recommended roads	
Other roads	
Restricted roads	
Buildings of interest	Hospital
Car Parks	P
Parks and open spaces	
Churches	†
One way streets	→

Area Plan

A roads	
B roads	
Stations	New Cross ●→
Borough Boundary	

Street Index with Grid Reference

Dalston/Hackney

Alvington Crescent	B3
Amhurst Road	C4-C3-D3-E3-E2
Andre Street	D4
Anton Street	D3-D4
Arcola Street	B4
Arundel Grove	A3
Balls Pond Road	A2-B2
Barrett's Grove	A4-B4
Beechwood Road	B1-B2
Belgrade Road	A4-B4
Belsham Street	F2
Bodney Road	D3-D4
Boleyn Road	A3-A2-B2
Brenthouse Road	E1-F1-F2
Brett Street	E3
Brickbeck Road	B2-B3
Buckingham Road	A1
Burder Road	A2
Cecilia Road	C3-C4

Chatham Place	F2
Churchill Walk	F3-F4
Clapton Square	E4-F4
Clarence Place	E4
Clarence Road	E3-E4
Colverstone Crescent	B2-B3-C3
Cowper Road	A4
Cresset Road	F2
Crossway	A3-B3
Culford Road	A1-A2
Dalston Lane	B2-C2-C3-D3-E3
Darnley Road	E1-E2-F2
De Beavoir Road	A1
Downs Park Road	B3-C3-C4-D4-E4
Dunn Street	B3-B4
Eleanor Road	D2-D1-E1
Ellingfort Road	E1
Elrington Road	C1-C2
Elsdale Street	F1-F2
Elton Place	A3
Engleford Road	A1-B1
Fasset Road	C2-D2
Fasset Square	C2
Ferncliffe Road	C3-C4
Forest Road	B1-C1-D1
Frampton Park Road	F1-F2
Gayhurst Road	C1-D1
Glenarm Road	F4
Gillette Street	A3-B3
Goulton Road	E4-F4
Graham Road	C2-D2-E2
Green Wood Road	D1-D2-D3
Hertford Road	A1
Hindrey Road	E3-E4
Holly Street	B1
Horton Road	D2-E2-E1
Kenmure Road	C3
King Henry Street	A3
King Henry's Walk	A2-A3
Kingsland High Street	B2-B3-B4
Kingsland Road	B1-B2
Kingsbury Road	A2
Landsdowne Drive	D1-D2
Laurel Street	B2-C2
Lentham Road	C1
Lesbia Road	F4
Loddiges Road	E1-F1
London Lane	E1
Lower Clapton Road	E3-E4-F4
Malvern Road	C1
Mapledene Road	C1-D1
Mare Street	E1-E2-E3
Martello Street	E1

Hackney / Dalston

Not so long ago this was a rural area on the west bank of the River Lea. Although most of its open land was swallowed up by development in the 19th century, pleasant spaces still remain in Hackney Downs, in the north, and London Fields, in the south, and attractive parks have been created.

The only old building of note is the ancient tower of St Augustine's Church, probably dating from the 13th century. This is a good area for street markets, one of the largest being on Saturdays, along busy Kingsland Road.

Stoke Newington was once the home of *Robinson Crusoe* author Daniel Defoe, and his house can still be seen in Stoke Newington Church Street — one of a number of reminders of the past to be found in this area. This old Saxon settlement became a fashionable residential area during the 19th century, but was extensively rebuilt following bomb damage in World War II. The Old Church of St Mary makes a picturesque scene at one corner of pleasantly landscaped Clissold Park.

Whitechapel was the scene of the notoriously grisly Jack the Ripper murders in the late 19th century. Famous also for its markets, which include Petticoat Lane (Middlesex Street), it has been a stopping point for immigrants since the 18th century. The National Museum of Labour History can be seen at nearby Limehouse Town Hall.

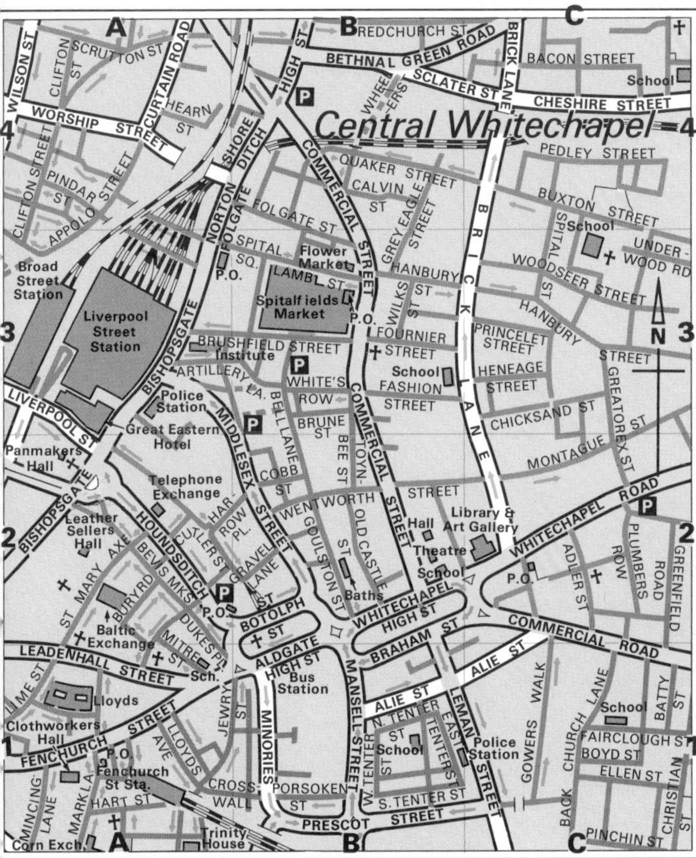

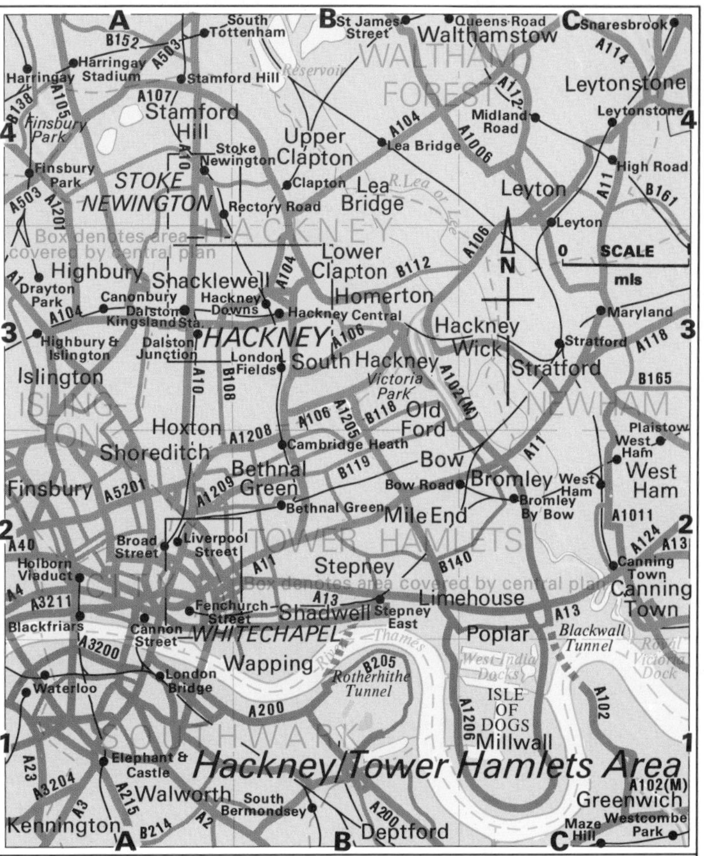

Mathias Road	A4
Mead Place	F1-F2
Median Road	F4
Mehetabel Road	F3
Mildmay Road	A3
Miller Avenue	B4
Montague Road	C3
Morning Lane	E2-F2
Mountford Road	C3
Navarino Road	D1-D2-D3
Palatine Road	A4-B4
Paragon Road	E2-F2
Parkholme Road	C1-C2
Pellerin Road	A3-A4
Pembury Road	D3-D4-E4
Ponsford Street	F2-F3
Powerscroft Road	F4
Prince George Road	A4-B4
Princess May Road	A4-B4
Queensbridge Road	C1-C2
Ram Place	F2
Ramsgate Street	B2
Reading Lane	E1-E2
Retreat Place	F2
Richmond Road	B1-C1-D1-E1
Ridley Road	B2-C2-C3
Ritson Road	C2
Roseberry Place	B1-B2
St Jude Street	A3
St Marks Rise	B2-B3
St Phillips Road	C1-C2
St Thomas Place	F1
Sandringham Road	B3-C3-D3
Seal Street	B4
Shacklewell Lane	B3-B4-C4
Shacklewell Street	B4-C4
Shellness Road	E4
Sigdon Road	D3
Sladen Place	E4
Somerford Grove	B4
Spenser Grove	A4
Spurstone Terrace	D3
Stamford Road	A1-B1
Stoke Newington Road	B3-B4
Sutton Place	F3
Sylvester Road	E2
Tilia Road	E4
Tolsford Road	E3
Tottenham Road	A2-A1-B1
Trumans Road	A3-B3
Urswich Road	F3-F4
Vallette Street	E2
Wayland Avenue	D3
Well Street	F1
Wilman Grove	D1
Wilton Way	C2-D2-E2
Wordsworth Road	A4

Stoke Newington

Alconbury Road	C3
Alkham Road	B3-B4
Amhurst Road	B1-C1
Batley Road	B2
Bayston Road	C2
Beatty Road	A1
Belfast Road	B4
Benthall Road	C2-C3
Bouverie Road	A3
Brighton Road	A1
Brodia Road	A2-A3
Brooke Road	B2-B3-C3
Cazenove Road	B4-C4
Chesholme Road	A2
Clapton Way	C1
Darville Road	B2
Defoe road	A2-A3
Downs Road	C1
Dumont Road	A3
Durlston Road	C3-C4
Dynevor Road	A2-A3
Evering Road	B1-B2-C2
Farleigh Road	B1
Filey Avenue	B4-C4
Foulden Road	B1-C1
Fountayne Road	C3-C4
Garnham Street	B3
Geldeston Road	C3
Hollar Road	B2
Jenner Road	B3-C3-C2
Kersley Road	A2-A3
Kynaston Road	A2-A3
Kyverdale Road	B3-B4-C4-B4
Lavers Road	A2
Leswin Road	B1-B2
Listria Park	A4
Manor Road	A4-B4
Manse Road	B1-C1
Maury Road	C2-C3
Nevill Road	A1-A2
Norcott Road	C2-C3
Northwold Road	B3-C3
Old Field Road	A1-A2-A3
Osbaldeston Road	C3-C4
Rectory Road	B3-B2-C2-C1
Rendlesham Road	C1-C2
Stamford Terrace	B3
Stamford Hill	B3-B4
Stoke Newington Church Street	A3-B3
Stoke Newington Common	B3-C3
Stoke Newington High Street	A2-B2-B3
Stoke Newington Road	A1
Sydner Road	B1-C1
Tyssen Road	B2
Victorian Grove	A2
Victorian Road	A1
Walford Road	A1
Windus Road	B4
Yorkshire Close	A2

Whitechapel

Adler Street	C2
Aldgate High Street	B1-B2
Alie Street	B1-C1-C2
Appolo Street	A3-A4
Artillery Lane	A3-B3
Back Church Lane	C1
Bacon Street	C4
Batty Street	C1
Bell Lane	B2-B3
Bethnal Green Road	B4-C4
Bevis Marks	A2
Bishopsgate	A2-A3
Boyd Street	C1
Braham Street	B1-B2-C2
Brick Lane	C2-C3-C4
Brune Street	B3
Brushfield Street	A3-B3
Bury Road	A2
Buxton Street	C3-C4
Calvin Street	B4
Cheshire Street	C4
Chicksand Street	C3
Christian Street	C1
Clifton Street	A3-A4
Cobb Street	B2
Commercial Road	C1-C2
Commercial Street	B2-B3-B4
Crosswall	A1-B1
Curtain Road	A4
Cutler Street	A2
Dukes Place	A1-A2
East Tenter Street	B1
Ellen Street	C1
Fairclough Street	C1
Fashion Street	B3
Fenchurch Street	A1
Folgate Street	B3-B4
Fournier Street	B3
Goulston Street	B2
Gowers Walk	C1-C2
Gravel Lane	B2
Greatorex Street	C2-C3
Greenfield Road	C1-C2
Grey Eagle Street	B3-B4
Hanbury Street	B3-C3-B3
Harrow Place	A2-B2
Hart Street	A1
Hearn Street	A4
Heneage Street	C3
High Street	B4
Houndsditch	A2-B2-B1-A2
Jewry Street	A1-B1
Lamb Street	B3
Leadenhall Street	A1
Leman Street	B1-C1
Lime Street	A1
Liverpool Street	A2-A3
Lloyds Avenue	A1
Mansell Street	B1
Mark Lane	A1
Middlesex Street	A3-A2-B2
Mincing Lane	A1
Minories	B1
Mitre Street	A1-A2
Montague Street	C2-C3
North Tenter Street	B1
Norton Folgate	A3-A4-B4
Old Castle Street	B2
Pedley Street	C4
Pinchin Street	C1
Pindar Street	A4
Plumbers Row	C2
Porsoken Street	B1
Prescot Street	B1-C1
Princelet Street	C3
Quaker Street	B4-C4
Redchurch Street	B4-C4
St Botolph Street	B2
St Mary Axe	A2
Sclater Street	B4-C4
Scrutton Street	A4
Shoreditch	B4
South Tentor Street	B1
Spital Square	A3-B3
Spital Street	C3-C4
Toynbee Street	B2-B3
Underwood Road	C3
Wentworth Street	B2-C2
West Tentor Street	B1
Wheeler Street	B4
Whitechapel High Street	B2
Whitechapel Road	C2
White's Row	B3
Wilks Street	B3
Wilson Street	A4
Woodseer Street	C3
Worship Street	A4

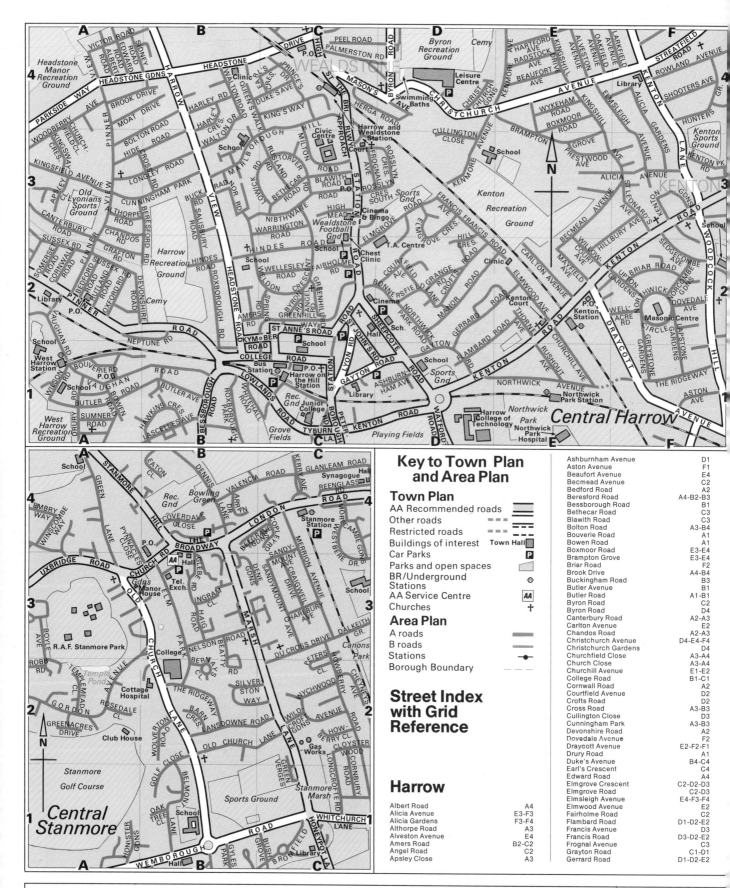

Key to Town Plan and Area Plan

Town Plan

AA Recommended roads	═══
Other roads	━━━
Restricted roads	┅┅┅
Buildings of interest	Town Hall ▢
Car Parks	P
Parks and open spaces	▨
BR/Underground Stations	⊖
AA Service Centre	AA
Churches	†

Area Plan

A roads	━━━
B roads	━━
Stations	●━
Borough Boundary	┅┅┅

Street Index with Grid Reference

Harrow

Albert Road	A4
Alicia Avenue	E3-F3
Alicia Gardens	F3-F4
Althorpe Road	A3
Alveston Avenue	E4
Amers Road	B2-C2
Angel Road	C2
Apsley Close	A3

Ashburnham Avenue	D1
Aston Avenue	F1
Beaufort Avenue	E4
Becmead Avenue	C2
Bedford Road	A4
Beresford Road	A4-B2-B3
Bessborough Road	B1
Bethecar Road	C3
Blawith Road	C3
Bolton Road	A3-B4
Bouverie Road	A1
Bowen Road	A1
Boxmoor Road	E3-E4
Brampton Grove	E3-E4
Briar Road	F2
Brook Drive	A4-B4
Buckingham Road	B3
Butler Avenue	B1
Butler Road	A1-B1
Byron Road	C2
Byron Road	D4
Canterbury Road	A2-A3
Carlton Avenue	E2
Chandos Road	A2-A3
Christchurch Avenue	D4-E4-F4
Christchurch Gardens	D4
Churchfield Close	A3-A4
Church Close	A3-A4
Churchill Avenue	E1-E2
College Road	B1-C1
Cornwall Road	A2
Courtfield Avenue	D2
Crofts Road	D2
Cross Road	A3-B3
Cullington Close	D3
Cunningham Park	A3-B3
Devonshire Road	A2
Dovedale Avenue	F2
Draycott Avenue	E2-F2-F1
Drury Road	A1
Duke's Avenue	B4-C4
Earl's Crescent	C4
Edward Road	A4
Elmgrove Crescent	C2-D2-D3
Elmgrove Road	C2-D3
Elmsleigh Avenue	E4-F3-F4
Elmwood Avenue	E2
Fairholme Road	C2
Flambard Road	D1-D2-E2
Francis Avenue	D3
Francis Road	D3-D2-E2
Frognal Avenue	C3
Grayton Road	C1-D1
Gerrard Road	D1-D2-E2

Harrow

Sheridan, Byron, Anthony Trollope and Sir Winston Churchill all spent time in Harrow — as pupils at the historic public school, which was founded in 1572. During term time, the present-day pupils are recognisable by their distinctive uniform, and tail coats are still worn by members of the Upper School. The school itself has been modernised to some extent over the years, but a number of ancient buildings still remain, notably the 17th-century schoolroom.

Expanded and developed between the two World Wars, modern Harrow is home of a number of industrial concerns, including the Kodak film and photographic paper factory and the Northern European Office of Hitachi Electronics.

St Mary's Church is of Norman origin but was greatly restored by Sir George Gilbert Scott during the mid-19th century. Headstone Manor, which dates back to the 14th century, has an impressive restored Tithe Barn which is open to the public.

Stanmore Marconi Space and Defence Systems is one of the occupants of Stanmore's main industrial estate, and as well as such modern innovations, the area still has some older buildings, including fine 18th-century houses on Stanmore Hill. St Lawrence's Church, also 18th-century, is noted for its painted walls and ceiling.

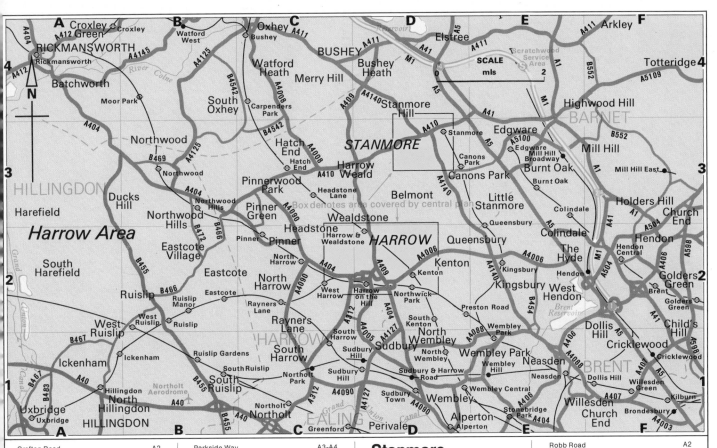

Grafton Road	A2	Parkside Way	A3-A4	
Grange Road	D2	Peel Road	C4-D4	
Greenhill Road	C2	Peterborough Road	C1	
Greenhill Way	C2	Pinner Road	A2-B1-B2	
Greystone Gardens	F1-F2	Pinner View	A2-A3-A4	
Harley Crescent	B3-B4	Prestwood Avenue	E3	
Harley Road	B4	Prince's Drive	B4-C4	
Harrow View	B2-B3-B4	Queen's Walk	B4-C4-C3	
Hartford Avenue	E4	Radnor Road	B3	
Hawkins Crescent	B1	Radstock Avenue	E4	
Headstone Drive	B4-C4	Rail Approach	C3-C4	
Headstone Gardens	A4-B4	Rosslyn Crescent	D3	
Headstone Road	B1-B2	Rosslyn Crescent South	C3-D3	
Herga Road	C4-D4	Rowland Avenue	F4	
Hide Road	A3-B3	Roxborough Park	B1	
High Mead	C3	Roxborough Road	B1-B2	
High Street	C4	Rushout Avenue	E1	
Hill Crescent	D2-D3	Rusland Road	C3	
Hillbury Avenue	E2-E3-F3	Rutland Road	A2	
Hindes Road	B2-C2	St Anne's Road	C2	
Hunters Grove	F4	St John's Road	C2-C1-D1	
Kenmore Avenue	D3-D4-E4	St Leonard's Avenue	F3	
Kenton Gardens	F3	Salisbury Road	B2-B3	
Kenton Lane	F3-F4	Sedgecombe Avenue	F2-F3	
Kenton Road	C1-D1-E1-E2-F2-F3	Sheepcote Road	D1-C2-D2	
Kenton Park Road	F3	Shooters Avenue	F4	
King's Way	C4	Sidney Road	A4	
Kingsfield Avenue	A3	Somerset Road	A2	
Kingshill Avenue	E4-E3-F3	Spring Road	F4	
Kingshill Drive	E4	Streatfield Road	F4	
Kingsway Crescent	A3	Station Road	C1-C2-C3	
Kymber Road	B1-B2-C2	Summer Road	A1	
Lascelles Avenue	B1	Sussex Road	A2-A3	
Lapstone Gardens	F1-F2	The Bridge	C4	
Larkfield Avenue	E4-F4	The Ridgeway	F1	
Longley Road	A3-B3	Thorne Avenue	E2	
Lowick Road	B3-C3	Torver Road	C3	
Lowlands Road	B1-C1	Tyburn Lane	C1	
Lyon Road	C1-C2	Upton Gardens	F2	
Manor Road	D2-E2	Vaughan Road	A1-A2-B1	
Marlborough Hill	B3-C3-C4	Victory Road	A4	
Mason's Avenue	C4-D4	Walton Drive	B3-B4	
Mayfield Avenue	E2	Walton Road	B4	
Milton Road	C3-C4	Warrington Road	B3-C3	
Moat Drive	A4-B4	Watford Road	D1	
Neptune Road	A2-B2	Weldon Crescent	B2-C2	
Nibthwaite Road	B3-C3	Wellacre Road	F2	
Norcombe Gardens	F2	Wellesley Road	C2	
Northwick Avenue	D1-E1	Whitehall Road	B1-C1	
Northwick Circle	F2	Willow Court Avenue	E2	
Northwick Park Road	D1-D2	Wilson Road	A1	
Oakfield Avenue	E4	Woodberry Avenue	A3-A4	
Oxford Road	A2	Woodcock Hill	F1-F2-F3	
Palmerston Road	C4-D4	Wykeham Road	E4	

Stanmore

Arron Drive	B4	Robb Road	A2	
Barn Crescent	B2	Rosedale Close	A2	
Beatty Road	B2-C3	Sandymount Avenue	C3-C4	
Belgrave Gardens	B4-C4	Silverston Way	B2-C2	
Belmont Lane	B1-B2	Stanmore Hill	A4-B4	
Bernays Close	B2	Templemead Close	A2	
Boyle Avenue	A2-A3	The Broadway	B4	
Bromfield	C1	The Ridgeway	B2	
Bush Grove	C1	Uxbridge Road	A3	
Charlbury Avenue	C3	Valencia Road	B4-C4	
Cheyney's Avenue	C2	Wemborough Road	A1-B1-C1	
Church Road	A3-B3-B4	Westbere Drive	C3-C4	
Cloyster Wood	C2	Whitchurch Lane	C1	
Copley Road	C4	Wildcroft Gardens	C2	
Cornbury Road	C1-C2	Winscombe Way	A4	
Coverdale Close	B4	Wolverton Road	B2	
Craigweil Drive	C3	Wychwood Avenue	C2	
Dalkeith Grove	C3			
Dene Gardens	B3-C3			
Dennis Lane	B4			
Du Cross Drive	C2-C3			
Eaton Close	B4			
Elm Park	B2-B3			
Embry Way	A4			
Glanleam Road	C4			
Glebe Road	B3-B4			
Golf Close	B1-B2			
Gordon Avenue	A2-A3-B3			
Green Lane	A3-A4			
Green Verges	C1-C2			
Greenacres Drive	A2			
Gyles Park	B1			
Haig Road	B3			
Honeypot Lane	C1			
Honister Gardens	A1			
Howberry Close	C2			
Howberry Road	C1-C2-C3			
Ingram Close	B3			
Kerry Avenue	C4			
Lansdowne Road	B2-C2			
London Road	B4-C4			
Longcrofte Road	C1-C2			
Marsh Lane	B4-B3-C3-C2-C1			
Merrion Avenue	C3-C4			
Morecambe Gardens	C3-C4			
Nelson Road	B3			
Oak Tree Close	B1			
Old Church Lane	A3-B3-B2-C2			
Peters Close	C2-C3			
Pynnacles Close	A4-A3-B3			
Reenglass Road	C4			

HARROW
The Old School building, Harrow School, whose 1572 founder John Lyon drew up an elaborate pupils' reading list of Latin and Greek — but no English — books, and stipulated that no girls be received into the school.

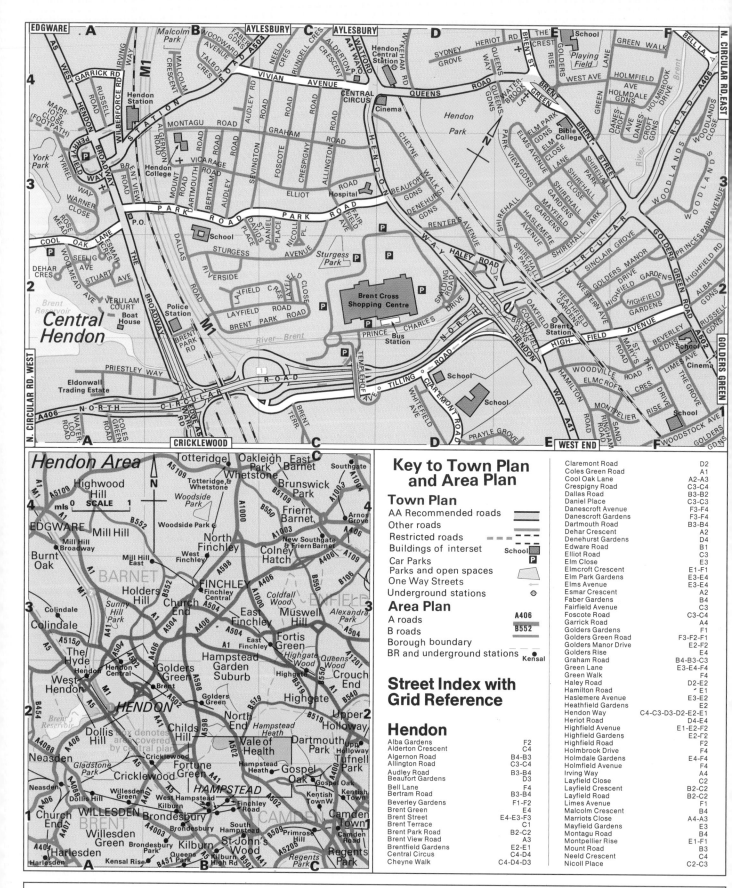

Hendon

The magnificent RAF Museum is situated here, next to Hendon Aerodrome (once famous for its air displays) which is also the site of the Battle of Britain and Bomber Command Museum. People flock to Hendon for these — and for the vast regional shopping centre at Brent Cross. Other local landmarks are the Metropolitan Police Training College and the Church Farm House Museum.

But Hendon is probably best known to the world for its closeness to the M1 Motorway, which has its southern terminal close by, near to the Staples Corner Junction on the North Circular road.

Hampstead Artists, poets and politicians have made their homes in Hampstead, where the celebrated Heath stretches for 800 acres of grass and woodland. Fine 17th- to 19th-century houses can be found in the 'village', and the stylish shops of Heath Street and Hampstead High Street add to the colourful atmosphere.

Outstanding buildings open to the public are Keats House (1815), home of the poet John Keats, Fenton House, which is a fine late 17th-century building, and Kenwood House, remodelled in about 1765 by Robert Adam and visited for its paintings and open-air concerts. Noted pubs of Hampstead include the Old Bull and Bush (the original for the music-hall song), the Flask, the Spaniards and Jack Straw's Castle.

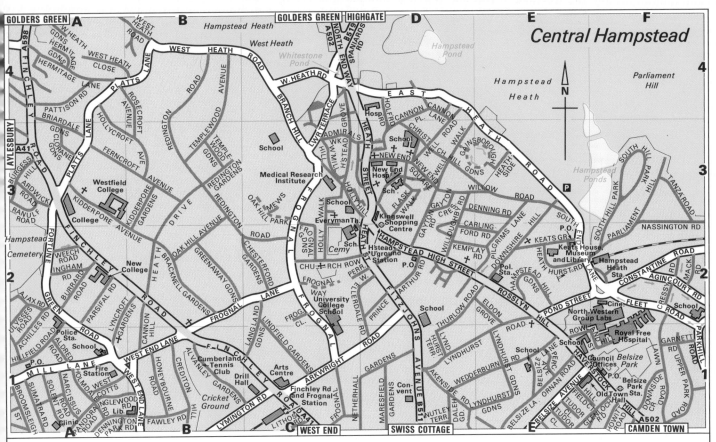

Central Hampstead

GOLDERS GREEN · GOLDERS GREEN · HIGHGATE · CAMDEN TOWN · WEST END · SWISS COTTAGE

Hampstead

(index)

North Circular Road	A1-B1-C1-D1-D2-E2-E3-F3-F4
Oakfield Court	E2
Park Road	A3-B3-C3-D3
Park View Gardens	E3-E4
Perryfield Way	A3
Prayle Grove	D1-E1
Priestley Way	A1-B1
Prince Charles Drive	C2-D2
Princes Park Avenue	F2-F3
Queens Gardens	E4
Queens Road	D4-E4
Queens Way	D4-E4
Renter's Avenue	D3-D2
Riverside	B2
Rose Mead	A3-A2
Rundell Crescent	C4
Russel Gardens	F2
Russel Road	A4
St Davids Place	B3-B2
St Marys Road	F1-F2
Sandringham Road	E1-F1
Seelig Avenue	A2
Sevington Road	B3-C3-C4
Shirehall Close	E3
Shirehall Gardens	E3
Shirehall Grove	E2-F2-F3
Shirehall Lane	E2-E3
Shirehall Park	E2-E3
Spalding Road	D2
Station Road	A3-A4-B2
Stuart Avenue	A2
Sturgess Avenue	B2-C2
Sydney Grove	D4
Talbot Crescent	B4
Templehof Avenue	C1-D1
The Broadway	A4-A3-A2-B2-B1
The Crest	E4
The Drive	F2-F1
The Grove	F1
Tilling Road	C1-D1-D2
Tyrrel Way	A3
Verulam Court	A2
Vicarage Road	B3
Vivian Avenue	B4-C4
Warner Close	A3
Waterbrook Lane	E4
Waterloo Road	A1
Watford Way	C4
West Avenue	E4
Western Avenue	E2-F2
Whitefield Avenue	D2
Wilberforce Road	A3-A4
Woodlands	F3-F4

Woodlands Close	F3-F4
Woodville Road	E1-F1
Woodward Avenue	B4
Woolmead Avenue	A2
Wykeham Road	D4

Hampstead

Achilles Road	A1-A2
Admirals Walk	C3-D3
Agincourt Road	F2
Ajax Road	A2
Akenside Road	D1
Aldred Road	A1
Alvanley Gardens	B1
Ardwick Road	A3
Arkwright Road	C1-D1-D2
Belsize Avenue	E1
Balsize Lane	E1
Bracknell Gardens	B2
Branch Hill	C4-C3
Briardale Gardens	A4-A3
Broomsleigh Street	A1
Burgess Hill	A3
Burnard Road	A2
Cannon Hill	B1-B2
Cannon Lane	D4-D3
Cannon Place	D3-D4
Carlingford Road	D2-E2
Chesterford Gardens	C2
Christchurch Hill	D3-E3
Church Row	C2
Clorane Gardens	A3
Constantine Road	F2
Crediton Hill	B1
Cressy Road	F2
Daleham Gardens	D1
Denning Road	D3-E3
Dennington Park Road	A1-B1
Downshire Hill	E2-E3
Downside Crescent	F1
East Heath Road	C4-D4-E4-E3-F3
Eklon Grove	E2
Ellerdale Road	C2-D1-D2
Fawley Road	B1
Ferncroft Avenue	A3-B3
Finchley Road	A4-A3-A2-B2-B1-C1
Fitzjohns Avenue	D2-D1
Flask Walk	F2-F1
Fleet Road	F2-F1
Fortune Green Road	A3-A2-A1
Frognal	C3-C2-C1
Frognal Close	C2

Frognal Gardens	C2-C3
Frognal Lane	B1-B2-C2
Frognal Way	C2
Gainsborough Gardens	D3-E3
Garnett Road	F1
Gayton Crescent	D3
Gayton Road	D2-D3
Glenloch Road	E1-F1
Greenaway Gardens	B2
Hampstead Grove	C3-C4
Hampstead Hill Gardens	E2
Hampstead High Street	D2-E2
Haverstock Hill	E1-F1
Heath Drive	B2-B3
Heath Street	C4-D4-D3-D2
Heath Hurst Road	E2
Heathside	D3
Hermitage Gardens	A4
Hermitage Lane	A4
Hillfield Court	E1-F1
Hillfield Road	A1-A2
Holford Road	D4-D3
Holly Hill	C3-D3
Holly Walk	C2-C3
Hollycroft Avenue	A4-A3-B3
Holmdale Road	A1
Honeybourne Road	B1
Hewitt Road	F1
Ingham Road	A2
Inglewood Road	A1-B1
Keats Grove	E2
Kemplay Road	D2-E2
Kidderpore Avenue	A3-A2-B2
Kidderpore Gardens	B2-B3
Langland Gardens	C1-C2
Lawn Road	F1
Lindfield Gardens	C1-C2
Lithos Road	C1
Lower Terrace	C3-C4
Lymington Road	B1-C1
Lyncroft Gardens	A1-A2-B2
Lyndhurst Gardens	D1-E1
Lyndhurst Grove	E1
Lyndhurst Road	D1-E1-E2
Lyndhurst Terrace	D1
Mackeson Road	F2
Maresfield Gardens	D1
Mill Lane	A1
Narcissus Road	A1
Nassington Road	F2-F3
Netherhall Gardens	C1-D1
New End	D3
New End Walk	D3
North End Way	C4

Nutley Terrace	D1
Oak Hill Avenue	B2-B3
Oakhill Park	C3
Oakhill Park Mews	C3
Ornan Road	E1
Pandora Road	A1
Parkhill Road	F1
Parliament Hill	E2-E3
Parsifal Road	A2
Pattisons Lane	A3-A4-B4
Perceval Avenue	E1
Perrins Walk	C2-D2
Pilgrims Lane	E2-E3
Platts Lane	A3-A4-B4
Pond Street	E2-F2
Prince Arthur Road	D2
Ranulf Road	A3
Redington Gardens	B3
Redington Road	B4-B3-B2-C2
Rosecroft Avenue	A4-B4-B3
Rosslyn Hill	E2-E1
Rowland Hill Street	E1-F1
Solent Road	A1
South End Lane	E3-E2-F2
South Hill Park	F2-F3
Spaniards Road	C4-D4
Sumatra Road	A1
Tanza Road	F3
Templewood Avenue	B3-B4
Templewood Gardens	B3
Thurlow Road	D1-D2-E2
Tudor Close	E1
Ulysses Road	A1
Upper Park Road	F1
Wedderburn Road	D1-E1
Weech Road	A2
Well Road	D3-D4
Well Walk	D3
West Cottages	A1
West End Lane	A1-B1
West Heath Close	A4-B4
West Heath Gardens	A4
West Heath Road	A4-B4-C4
Willoughby Road	D2-D3
Willow Road	D3-E3
Windmill Hill	C3

HAMPSTEAD
John Keats wrote *Ode to a Nightingale* while living at Wentworth Place (now Keats House) from 1818 to 1820. Books, letters and other mementoes of the poet and his fianceé, Fanny Brawne, can be seen here.

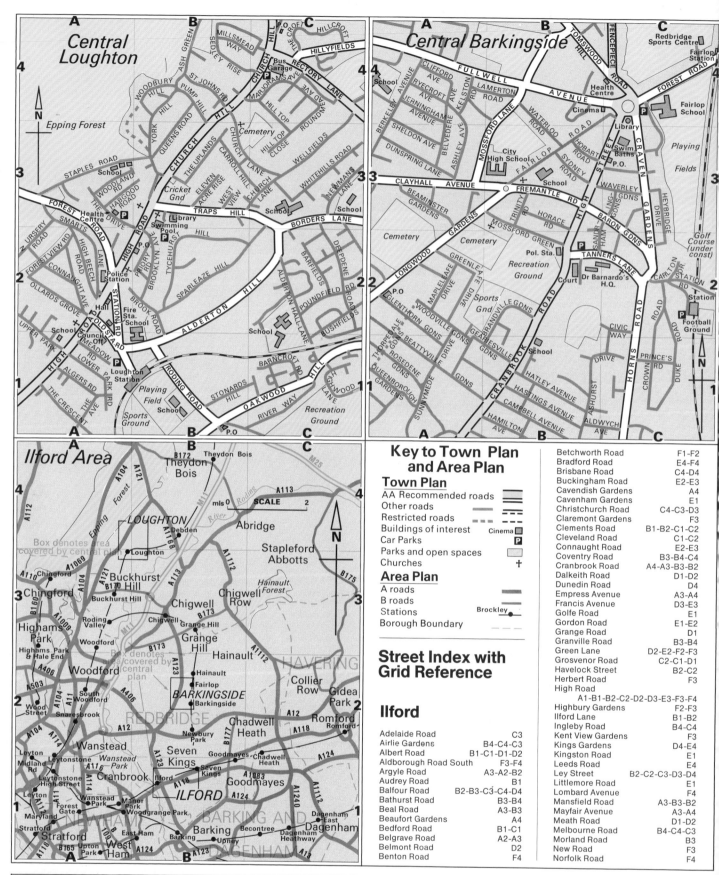

Key to Town Plan and Area Plan

Town Plan

AA Recommended roads	
Other roads	
Restricted roads	
Buildings of interest	Cinema
Car Parks	P
Parks and open spaces	
Churches	†

Area Plan

A roads	
B roads	
Stations	Brockley ●
Borough Boundary	

Street Index with Grid Reference

Ilford

Adelaide Road	C3
Airlie Gardens	B4-C4-C3
Albert Road	B1-C1-D1-D2
Aldborough Road South	F3-F4
Argyle Road	A3-A2-B2
Audrey Road	B1
Balfour Road	B2-B3-C3-C4-D4
Bathurst Road	B3-B4
Beal Road	A3-B3
Beaufort Gardens	A4
Bedford Road	B1-C1
Belgrave Road	A2-A3
Belmont Road	D2
Benton Road	F4

Betchworth Road	F1-F2
Bradford Road	E4-F4
Brisbane Road	C4-D4
Buckingham Road	E2-E3
Cavendish Gardens	A4
Cavenham Gardens	E1
Christchurch Road	C4-C3-D3
Claremont Gardens	F3
Clements Road	B1-B2-C1-C2
Cleveland Road	C1-C2
Connaught Road	E2-E3
Coventry Road	B3-B4-C4
Cranbrook Road	A4-A3-B3-B2
Dalkeith Road	D1-D2
Dunedin Road	D4
Empress Avenue	A3-A4
Francis Avenue	D3-E3
Golfe Road	E1
Gordon Road	E1-E2
Grange Road	D1
Granville Road	B3-B4
Green Lane	D2-E2-F2-F3
Grosvenor Road	C2-C1-D1
Havelock Street	B2-C2
Herbert Road	F3
High Road	A1-B1-B2-C2-D2-D3-E3-F3-F4
Highbury Gardens	F2-F3
Ilford Lane	B1-B2
Ingleby Road	B4-C4
Kent View Gardens	F3
Kings Gardens	D4-E4
Kingston Road	E1
Leeds Road	E4
Ley Street	B2-C2-C3-D3-D4
Littlemore Road	E1
Lombard Avenue	F4
Mansfield Road	A3-B3-B2
Mayfair Avenue	A3-A4
Meath Road	D1-D2
Melbourne Road	B4-C4-C3
Morland Road	B3
New Road	F3
Norfolk Road	F4

Ilford

Situated seven miles from London, Ilford is developing into a light industrial town with expanding industrial estates and a development programme to pedestrianise several important shopping streets. Valentines Park provides 130 acres of recreation area and includes peaceful havens such as the Old English Garden, the Rosary Terrace and Bishops Walk, as well as an ornamental pond and a lake. Set within the grounds of the park is one of the oldest buildings in the borough, Valentines House, which was built at the end of the 17th century.

Loughton's prominent Lopping Hall was built in 1884 by the City of London, after protests by local woodsmen about the lopping rights of the townspeople, and is now used for various community functions. Even today, the woodlands of Epping Forest dominate the town: Loughton stretches along its south-easterly side, and is bordered by the Rover Roding to the east. Interesting older buildings in the area include Loughton Hall and partly 16th-century Alderton Hall.

Barkingside is growing steadily due to recent business and housing developments and has a pleasant shopping area, various recreation grounds and the Redbridge Sports Centre. Fairlop Plain, just north of the town, is used for football, sailing and flying model aeroplanes.

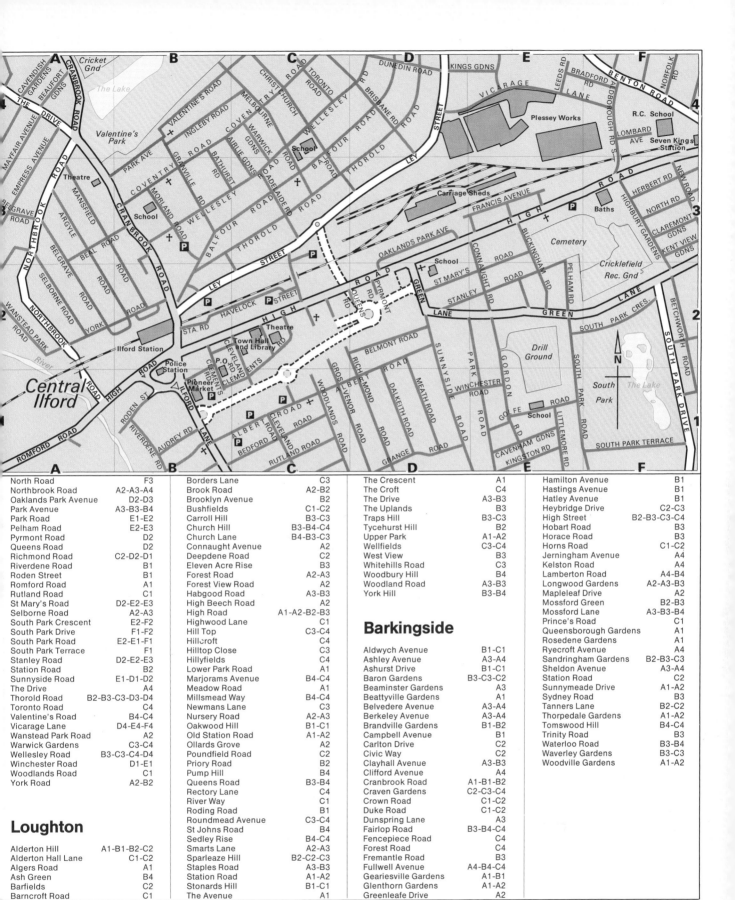

North Road	F3	Borders Lane	C3	The Crescent	A1	Hamilton Avenue	B1
Northbrook Road	A2-A3-A4	Brook Road	A2-B2	The Croft	C4	Hastings Avenue	B1
Oaklands Park Avenue	D2-D3	Brooklyn Avenue	B2	The Drive	A3-B3	Hatley Avenue	B1
Park Avenue	A3-B3-B4	Bushfields	C1-C2	The Uplands	B3	Heybridge Drive	C2-C3
Park Road	E1-E2	Carroll Hill	B3-C3	Traps Hill	B3-C3	High Street	B2-B3-C3-C4
Pelham Road	E2-E3	Church Hill	B3-B4-C4	Tycehurst Hill	B2	Hobart Road	B3
Pyrmont Road	D2	Church Lane	B4-B3-C3	Upper Park	A1-A2	Horace Road	B3
Queens Road	D2	Connaught Avenue	A2	Wellfields	C3-C4	Horns Road	C1-C2
Richmond Road	C2-D2-D1	Deepdene Road	C2	West View	B3	Jerningham Avenue	A4
Riverdene Road	B1	Eleven Acre Rise	B3	Whitehills Road	C3	Kelston Road	A4
Roden Street	B1	Forest Road	A2-A3	Woodbury Hill	B4	Lamberton Road	A4-B4
Romford Road	A1	Forest View Road	A2	Woodland Road	A3-B3	Longwood Gardens	A2-A3-B3
Rutland Road	C1	Habgood Road	A3-B3	York Hill	B3-B4	Mapleleaf Drive	A2
St Mary's Road	D2-E2-E3	High Beech Road	A2			Mossford Green	B2-B3
Selborne Road	A2-A3	High Road	A1-A2-B2-B3			Mossford Lane	A3-B3-B4
South Park Crescent	E2-F2	Highwood Lane	C1	**Barkingside**		Prince's Road	C1
South Park Drive	F1-F2	Hill Top	C3-C4			Queensborough Gardens	A1
South Park Road	E2-E1-F1	Hillcroft	C4	Aldwych Avenue	B1-C1	Rosedene Gardens	A1
South Park Terrace	F1	Hilltop Close	C3	Ashley Avenue	A3-A4	Ryecroft Avenue	A4
Stanley Road	D2-E2-E3	Hillyfields	C4	Ashurst Drive	B1-C1	Sandringham Gardens	B2-B3-C3
Station Road	B2	Lower Park Road	A1	Baron Gardens	B3-C3-C2	Sheldon Avenue	A3-A4
Sunnyside Road	E1-D1-D2	Marjorams Avenue	B4-C4	Beaminster Gardens	A3	Station Road	C2
The Drive	A4	Meadow Road	A1	Beattyville Gardens	A1	Sunnymeade Drive	A1-A2
Thorold Road	B2-B3-C3-D3-D4	Millsmead Way	B4-C4	Belvedere Avenue	A3-A4	Sydney Road	B3
Toronto Road	C4	Newmans Lane	C3	Berkeley Avenue	A3-A4	Tanners Lane	B2-C2
Valentine's Road	B4-C4	Nursery Road	A2-A3	Brandville Gardens	B1-B2	Thorpedale Gardens	A1-A2
Vicarage Lane	D4-E4-F4	Oakwood Hill	B1-C1	Campbell Avenue	B1	Tomswood Hill	B4-C4
Wanstead Park Road	A2	Old Station Road	A1-A2	Carlton Drive	C2	Trinity Road	B3
Warwick Gardens	C3-C4	Ollards Grove	A2	Civic Way	C2	Waterloo Road	B3-B4
Wellesley Road	B3-C3-C4-D4	Poundfield Road	C2	Clayhall Avenue	A3-B3	Waverley Gardens	B3-C3
Winchester Road	D1-E1	Priory Road	B2	Clifford Avenue	A4	Woodville Gardens	A1-A2
Woodlands Road	C1	Pump Hill	B4	Cranbrook Road	A1-B1-B2		
York Road	A2-B2	Queens Road	B3-B4	Craven Gardens	C2-C3-C4		
		Rectory Lane	C4	Crown Road	C1-C2		
		River Way	C1	Duke Road	C1-C2		
		Roding Road	B1	Dunspring Lane	A3		
Loughton		Roundmead Avenue	C3-C4	Fairlop Road	B3-B4-C4		
		St Johns Road	B4	Fencepiece Road	C4		
Alderton Hill	A1-B1-B2-C2	Sedley Rise	B4-C4	Forest Road	C4		
Alderton Hall Lane	C1-C2	Smarts Lane	A2-A3	Fremantle Road	B3		
Algers Road	A1	Sparleaze Hill	B2-C2-C3	Fullwell Avenue	A4-B4-C4		
Ash Green	B4	Staples Road	A3-B3	Geariesville Gardens	A1-B1		
Barfields	C2	Station Road	A1-A2	Glenthorn Gardens	A1-A2		
Barncroft Road	C1	Stonards Hill	B1-C1	Greenleafe Drive	A2		
		The Avenue	A1				

ILFORD
A resplendent turn-of-the-century Town Hall epitomises the confidence felt by those who fostered Ilford's expansion — one of them guaranteed season ticket sales worth £10,000 when a station opened here in 1889.

Islington

Taverns and amusements made Islington a fashionable residential area and place of entertainment during the 18th century. Its theatrical traditions are carried on today by Sadler's Wells Theatre, dating from the 17th century and now home of the Sadler's Wells Royal Ballet Company. Cannonbury Tower is a much restored former manor house which is now in use as

a theatre, and also worth a visit are the antique shops and market stalls of Camden Passage.

Wood Green has become synonymous in North London with Shopping City, an extensive complex which was officially opened in 1981, and also houses the New River Sports Centre. Once a rural hamlet, Wood Green is now the administrative centre for the London Borough of Haringey.

Holloway is noted for the Sobell Sports Centre, said to be the largest in the country. The

Arsenal Football Club is another feature of the local landscape.

Tottenham Rivalling its nearby neighbours Tottenham Hotspur Football Club has its ground here — probably the most widely known aspect of this part-industrial, mainly residential area, which was once an agricultural community on the River Lea. There are several pleasant parks, and Bruce Castle Park has a local museum in a partly-Elizabethan building.

LEGEND

Town Plan

- AA Recommended roads
- Other roads
- Restricted roads
- Buildings of interest — College
- Car Parks — P
- Parks and open spaces
- Churches — †
- BR and Underground Stations

Area Plan

- A roads
- B roads
- Stations — Stamford Hill
- Borough Boundary

STREET INDEX WITH GRID REFERENCE

WOOD GREEN

Acacia Road	C4
Alexandra Road	B2
Bedford Road	A4
Bounds Green Road	A4-B4
Braemar Avenue	A4
Brook Road	B3
Buckingham Road	A4
Burghley Road	B2
Bury Road	B2-C2
Carlingford Road	C1
Church Lane	A1
Claredon Road	A2-B2
Cobham Road	C2
Coburg Road	A3-B3
Cranbrook Park	B4
Cross Lane	A1-A2
Darwin Road	C3
Dorset Road	A4
Dunbar Road	C4
Ewart Grove	B4
Falkland Road	B1-C1
Farrant Avenue	B3-C3
Frobisher Road	B1-C1
Gathorne Road	B3
Gladstone Avenue	B3-C3
Glebe Road	A1
Green Lanes	C1-C2
Hampden Road	A1-B1
Hawke Park Road	C2
Hewitt Avenue	C2-C3
High Road	B4-B3-B2-C2
High Street	A1
Hillfield Avenue	A1
Hornsey Park Road	B2-B3
King's Road	B4
Langham Road	C1-C2
Lausanne Road	B1
Leith Road	C4
Lordship Lane	B3-C3-C4-C3
Lymington Avenue	B2-B3-C3
Lyttle Road	B2
Malvern Road	B2
Mannock Road	C2
Mayes Road	A3-B3
Meads Road	C2
Morley Avenue	B3-C3
Moselle Avenue	B3-C3
Park Avenue	A4
Park Ridings	B2-B3
Parkland Road	B3
Pelham Road	B3
Pellatt Grove	B4-C4
Perth Road	C4
Progress Way	C4
Raleigh Road	B1
Ravenstone Road	B2
Russell Avenue	C2-C3
Salisbury Road	C3
Selbourne Road	A4-B4
Sirdar Road	C2
Solway Road	C4
Stanmore Road	C1
Station Road	A4-A3-B3
Stirling Road	C4
Sydney Road	B1
The Avenue	B2
The Sandlings	B3-B2-C2
Tottenham Lane	A1
Trinity Road	A4-B4
Turnpike Lane	A1-B1-B2
Vincent Road	C3
Waldeck Road	C1
Watsons Road	B4
West Beech Road	B2-C2
Westbury Avenue	C2
Western Road	A2-A3
West Green Road	C1
White Hart Lane	B4-C4
Whymark Avenue	B2-C2
Wightman Road	B1
Willingdon Road	C2
Willoughby Road	B2-B1-C1
Winkfield Road	C3-C4

TOTTENHAM

Adams Road	A4
Antill Road	B1-B2-C2
Arnold Road	B2-B3
Ashby Road	B1
Ashley Road	C2-C3
Beaconsfield Road	A1-A2
Bedford Road	A1-A2
Braemar Road	A1
Broad Lane	B1-C1-C2
Broadwater Road	A4
Bruce Grove	A4-B4
Brunswick Road	A1
Buller Road	C3
Carew Road	C4
Chandos Road	A4
Chester Road	A3
Chestnut Road	B3-C3
Clyde Circus	A2
Clyde Road	A2-B2
Cunningham Road	B2-C2-C1
Dongola Road	A2-A3
Dowsett Road	B4-C4
Drayton Road	A3-A4
Elmhurst Road	A4-B4
Fairbanks Road	B2-B3
Fairbourne Road	A3
Farley Road	C2
Ferry Lane	C2
Forster Road	B3
Fountayne Road	C1
Greenfield Road	A1
Greyhound Road	A2-A3-B3
Griffin Road	A4
Grove Park Road	A1-A2
Hale Road	C2-C3
Hanover Road	B1-B2
Havelock Road	C4
High Road	B1-B2-B3-B4
Holcombe Road	B3-C3
Jansons Road	A2
Kimberley Road	C3-C4
Kirkton Road	A1
Kitchener Road	A2-A3
Ladysmith Road	B3-B4
Lawrence Road	A1-A2
Linley Road	A4
Lordsmead Road	A4
Mafeking Road	C4
Markfield Road	C1
Mitchley Road	B3-C3
Monument Way	B2-C2-C3
Morrison Avenue	A3
Mount Pleasant Road	A2-A3-A4
Napier Road	A3
Newlyn Road	B4
Page Green Terrace	B1
Park View Road	C3-C4
Pembury Road	B4
Phillip Lane	A2-B2
Portland Road	B1
Poynton Road	C4
Radley Road	A4
Ranelagh Road	A3
Rangemoor Road	B1
Reed Road	B3-B4
Roseberry Avenue	C4
Roslyn Road	A1
St Loy's Road	A3-B3
Scales Road	B3-C3
Seaford Road	A1
Seymour Avenue	B4-C4
Sherringham Avenue	B4-C4
Southey Road	A1
Sperling Road	A4-A3-B3
Springfield Road	B2-C2
Stamford Road	C1
Station Road	C2
Steele Road	A3-B3
Talbot Road	B1-B2
Tamar Way	B3-C3
Thackeray Avenue	C4
The Avenue	A3-A4-B4
The Hale	C2-C3
Tynemouth Road	B2-C2
Wakefield Road	B1
Westerfield Road	B1
West Green Road	A1-B1
Willan Road	A3-A4
Wimbourne Road	A4
Winchelsea Road	A2-A3-B3
Woodside Gardens	A3-A4-B4

HOLLOWAY

Alexandra Road	A3-A4
Ambler Road	C3-C4
Andover Road	A4-B4
Annette Road	B2
Arvon Road	C1
Ashburton Grove	B2-C2
Aubert Park	C2
Avenell Road	C2-C3
Axminster Road	A3-B3
Battledean Road	C1
Beacon Hill	A1
Benwell Road	B2-B1-C1
Berriman Road	B3
Biddestone Road	A2-B2
Birnham Road	A4-B4
Blackstock Road	C4
Bracey Street	A4
Briset Way	B4
Bryantwood Road	C1
Caledonian Road	A2-A1-B1
Camden Road	A1-A2
Cardozo Road	A1
Citizen Road	B2-B3
Clifton Terrace	B4
Corker Way	B3-B4
Cornwallis Road	A3-A4
Drayton Park	C1-C2-C3
Dunford Road	B2
Durham Road	B4
Eburne Road	A3
Eden Grove	B1
Elfort Road	C2-C3
Fieldway Crescent	C1
Finsbury Park Road	C4
Fonthill Road	B4-C4
Freegrove Road	A1
Georges Road	B1
Gillespie Road	C3
Hatley Road	B4
Hertslet Road	A3-A2-B2
Highbury Crescent	C1
Highbury Hill	C2-C3
Hillmarton Road	A1-B1
Holloway Road	A3-A2-B2-B1-C1
Hornsey Road	A4-A3-B3-B2-B1
Horsell Road	C1
Isledon Road	B3-C3-C4
Jackson Road	B2
Kingsdown Road	A4
Landseer Road	A3-A4
Lennox Road	B4
Lister Mews	B2
Liverpool Road	B1-C1
Loraine Road	B2
Lowman Road	B2
Manor Gardens	A3
Mayton Street	A3-B3
Medina Road	B3
Mingard Walk	A3-B3-B4
Moray Road	B4
Morgan Road	C1
Monsell Road	C3
Newington Barrow Way	B3-B4
Parkhurst Road	A1-A2
Penn Road	A1-A2
Plimsoll Road	C3-C4
Queens Drive	C4
Queensland Road	B2-C2
Quemerford Road	B1-B2
Rock Street	C4
Roden Street	A2-B2-B3
Romilly Road	C3-C4
Ronalds Road	C1
Roth Walk	B4
St Thomas's Road	C3-C4
Salterton Road	A3
Seven Sisters Road	A2-A3-B3-B4-C4
Stavordale Road	C2
Stock Orchard Crescent	B1
Sussex Way	A4-A3-B3
Tabley Road	A2
Thane Villas	B3
Tollington Park	A4-B4
Tollington Road	B2-B3
Tollington Way	A3-A4
Tufnell Park Road	A2-A3
Warlters Road	A2
Wells Terrace	B4-C4
Whistler Street	C1-C2
Widdenham Road	A2-B2-B1
Wilberforce Road	C4
Windsor Road	A3
Witherington Road	C1
Wray Crescent	A4
Yonge Park	B3

ISLINGTON

Almeida Street	B3
Amwell Street	A1
Baldwin Terrace	C2
Barford Street	B3
Barnsbury Park	A4-B4
Barnsbury Road	A2-A3
Barnsbury Square	A4
Barnsbury Street	A4-A3
Belitha Villas	A4
Baron Street	A1-A2
Bewdley Street	A4-B4
Bishop Street	C3
Braes Street	C4
Britannia Row	C3
Brooksbury Street	A4-B4
Burgh Street	C2
Camden Walk	B2
Canonbury Villas	C4
Canonbury Road	C4
Central Street	C1
Chadwell Street	B1
Chapel Market	A2-B2
Charlotte Terrace	A2-A3
City Garden Row	C1-C2
City Road	B1-C1
Clare Square	A1
Cloudesley Place	A2-B2
Cloudesley Road	A2-A3
Cloudesley Square	A3-B3
Cloudesley Street	A2-A3
Colebrooke Row	B1-B2-B3
College Cross	B4
Copenhagen Street	A2-A3
Cross Street	B3-C3
Cruden Street	C2-C3
Culpepper Street	A2
Dagmar Terrace	B3-C3
Danbury Street	C2
Devonia Street	B2-C2
Dewey Road	A2
Donegal Street	A1-A2
Duncan Street	B2
Duncan Terrace	B1-B2
Elia Street	B2-B1-C1
Essex Road	B2-B3-C3-C4
Florence Street	B3-B4
Friend Street	B1
Frome Street	C2
Gerrard Road	B2-C2
Gibson Square	B3
Goswell Road	B1-C1
Graham Street	C1-C2
Grant Street	A2
Green Man Street	C3-C4
Hall Street	C1
Halton Road	C3-C4
Hawes Street	B4-C4
Hemingford Road	A3-A4
High Street	B2
Islington Park Street	B4
Liverpool Road	B2-B3-B4
Lloyd Street	A1
Lofting Road	A4-B4
Lonsdale Square	A3-A4
Masons Place	C1
Milner Square	B3-B4
Moon Street	B3
Moreland Street	C1
Myddleton Square	A1-B1
New North Road	C4
Noel Road	B2-C2
Offord Road	A4
Packington Square	C2-C3
Packington Street	C3
Parkfield Street	B2
Penton Street	A1-A2
Pentonville Road	A1-B1
Percy Circus	A1
Percy Street	A1
Pleasant Place	C3-C4
Popham Street	C3
Prebend Street	C3
Raleigh Street	C2-C3
Rawstorne Street	B1
Rheidol Terrace	C2
Richmond Avenue	A3-B3
Richmond Crescent	A3
Ripplevale Grove	A3-A4
River Place	C4
River Street	A1
St John Street	B1
St Peters Street	B3-C3-C2
Sebbon Street	B4-C4
Stonefield Street	A3
Sudeley Street	B1-C1-C2
Theberton Street	B3
Thornhill Road	A3-A4
Upper Street	B2-B3-B4
Vincent Terrace	B2-C2
Wakley Street	B1
Wenlock Road	C1-C2
Wharf Road	C1-C2
White Lion Street	A2-B2

Kingston upon Thames Area

Central Kingston upon Thames

Kingston

Seven Saxon kings — at least — were crowned where the coronation stone now stands, near the Guildhall in the centre of town. Kingston kept up its connections with royalty, and they reached a peak in 1927 when George V confirmed its status as a Royal Borough.

Hampton Court, Kew Gardens and Richmond Park are all nearby. A number of ancient buildings can be seen in the High Street, and the Kingston Heritage Centre in Fairfield West is well worth a visit. A pleasant Thames-side setting, an extensive open-air market, the recently completed Eden Walk shopping precinct and a variety of old-established shops ensure Kingston's continued popularity.

Surbiton was chosen in preference to Kingston for the first local railway station in the 19th century, and rapidly grew in importance. A pleasant residential suburb, it has good entertainment facilities at the Assembly Rooms and the popular Surrey Grass Court Tennis Championships are held at Surbiton Lawn Tennis Club each year.

Epsom was already popular as a 'dormitory' town in the 18th century. Towards the end of that century, horse racing became popular on Epsom Downs, and the first Oaks was run here in 1779, followed by the first Derby in 1780. Modern Epsom is still mainly residential.

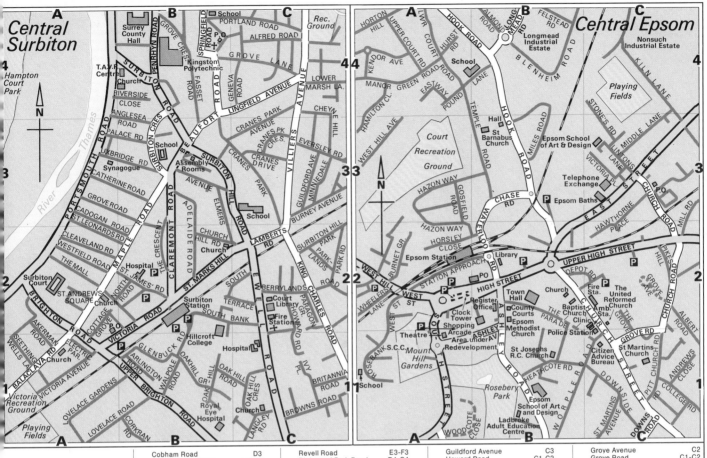

Central Surbiton

Central Epsom

LEGEND

Town Plan

- AA recommended route
- Restricted roads
- Other roads
- Buildings of interest
- Car parks
- Parks and open spaces

Area Plan

- A roads
- B roads
- Locations — Ockham○
- Urban area

Street Index with Grid Reference

Kingston Upon Thames

Acre Road	B4-C4
Albert Road	C2-C3
Alexandra Road	D4-E4
Alfred Road	C1
Arundel Road	F2-F3
Athelstan Road	C1-D1
Beechcroft Avenue	F2-F3
Beresford Road	C4-D4
Birkenhead Avenue	C3-D3
Blenheim Gardens	D2-E2
Bonner Hill Road	F3-F4
Brook Gardens	B2
Brook Street	B2
Brunswick Road	D4-E4
Burritt Road	D2-E2
Cambridge Road	D3-D2-E2
Canbury Park Road	C3-D3-D4
Cardinal Crescent	F3
Caversham Road	C2-C3
Charter Road	E2-F2
Chatham Road	D3
Chesham Road	D3
Church Grove	A3
Church Road	C2-C3-D3
Clarence Avenue	F2
Clarence Street	A3-B3
Clifton Road	D3-D4
Cobham Road	D3
Coombe Lane West	E3-F3
Coombe Rise	F3-F4
Coombe Road	D3-E3
Cranbury Avenue	C3-C4-D4
Craven Road	C4-D4
Cromwell Road	B3-C3
Dagmar Road	D4
Dawson Road	C1-D1-D2-C2
Deacon Road	C3-C4-D4
Denmark Road	B1-C1
Dickerage Lane	F1-F2
Dickerage Road	F2-F3
Douglas Road	E1-E2
Down Hall Road	B3
Ernest Road	E2
Eastbury Road	B4
East Road	B4-C4
Eden Street	B2-B3
Elm Crescent	C3-C4
Elm Grove	C3
Elm Road	C3-C4-D4
Elton Road	D2-E2
Fairfield East	C2-C3
Fairfield Place	C1
Fairfield Road	B2-C2
Fairfield South	C2
Fairfield West	B2-B3-C3
Fife Road	B3
Fleetwood Road	F1-F2
Galsworthy Road	E3-E4
Gibbon Road	B4-C4
Glamorgan Road	A4
Gloucester Road	E2-E3
Gordon Road	C3-D3
Grange Road	B2-B1-C1
Grove Crescent	B1
Grove Lane	B1-C1
Hampden Road	E1-E2
Hampton Court Road	A3
Hawks Road	C2-D2
High Street	A3
High Street	A1-A2-B2
Homersham Road	E3
Kenley Road	E3-F3-F2
King Henry's Road	E1-E2-F2
Kings Road	B4-C4
Kingston Hill	D3-D4-E4
Kingston Road	E2-E1-F1
Knights Park	B1-B2
Linden Grove	D2
London Road	B3-C3-D3
Lower Ham Road	B3-B4
Lower Teddington Road	A3-A4
Lowther Road	C4-D4
Manor Gate	D3-E3
Mill Place	C2
Mill Street	C1-C2
Milner Road	B1
Neville Road	E2-E3
Norbiton Avenue	E2-E3
Orchard Road	B2
Orme Road	E3-E2-F2
Park Road	D3-D4
Park Street	A3
Penrhyn Road	B1-B2
Piper Road	D2
Porchester Road	E2-F2
Portland Road	B1-C1
Portsmouth Road	A1-B1
Princes Road	D4
Queens Road	E4

Revell Road	E3-F3
Richmond Park Road	B4-C4
Richmond Road	B3-B4
Rosebery Road	E2
Rowells Road	D2
St James's Road	B2
St Johns Road	A3
Seymour Road	A3-A4
Somerset Road	D2
Springfield Road	B1
Station Road	A4
Station Road	D3
Surbiton Road	B1
Thames Side	B3
Thames Street	B2-B3
The Bittoms	B1-B2
The Triangle	F2
Union Street	B2-B3
Upper Teddington Road	A3-A4
Victoria Road	C2-D2
Villiers Road	C1-C2
Vincent Road	D2-E2
Waters Road	E2
Willingham Way	D2
Willoughby Road	D3-D4
Wolsey Close	F3-F4
Wolverton Avenue	E3-E4
Woodbines Avenue	B1
Wood Street	B3
York Road	D4

Surbiton

Adelaide Road	B2-B3
Akerman Road	A1-A2
Alfred Road	C4
Anglesea Road	A4-B4-B3
Arlington Road	B1
Avenue Elmers	C2-B2-B3
Balaclava Road	A1
Beaufort Road	B3-B4
Berrylands Road	C2
Brighton Road	A1-A2
Britannia Road	C1
Browns Road	C1
Burney Avenue	C3
Cadogan Road	A3-A2-B2
Catherine Road	A3-B3
Cheyne Hill	C3-C4
Church Hill Road	B2
Claremont Road	B2-B3
Cleaveland Road	A2
Corkran Road	B1
Cottage Grove	A1-A2
Cranes Drive	C3
Cranes Park	B3-C3
Cranes Park Avenue	B3-C3-C4
Cranes Park Crescent	C3
Electric Parade	A1
Eversley Road	C3
Ewell Road	C1-C2
Fasset Road	B3-B4
Geneva Road	B2
Glenbuck Road	B1-B2
Grove Crescent	B2
Grove Lane	B4-C4
Grove Road	A3-B3-B2

Guildford Avenue	C3
Howard Road	C1-C2
Ivy Place	C1
King Charles Road	C1-C2
Lamberts Road	C2
Langley Road	C1
Lingfield Avenue	B4-C4
Lovelace Gardens	A1-B1
Lovelace Road	A1-B1
Lower Marsh Lane	C4
Maple Road	A2-B2-B3
Minniedale	C3
North Road	A2-B2
Oakhill	B1
Oakhill Crescent	C1
Oakhill Grove	B1
Oakhill Road	B1-C1
Palace Road	A3-B3
Paragon Grove	C2
Parklands	C2
Park Road	C2
Penrhyn Road	B4
Portland Road	B4-C4
Portsmouth Road	A2-A3-A4
Riverside Close	A4-B4
St Andrews Square	A2
St James' Road	A2-B2
St Leonards Road	A3-A2-B2
St Marks Hill	B2-C2
Seething Wells Lane	A1-A2
South Bank	B2-C2
South Terrace	B2-C2
Springfield Road	B4
Surbiton Crescent	B3-B4
Surbiton Hill Park	B2
Surbiton Hill Road	B3-C3-C2
Surbiton Road	B3-B4
The Crescent	B2-B3
The Mall	A2
Upper Brighton Road	A1-B1
Uxbridge Road	A3-B3
Victoria Avenue	A1
Victoria Road	A1-B1-B2
Villiers Road	C2-C3-C4
Walpole Road	B1
Westfield Road	A2

Epsom

Albert Road	C1-C2
Almond Road	B4
Andrews Close	C1
Ashley Avenue	A1-B1
Ashley Road	B1-B2
Blenheim Road	B4
Burnet Grove	A2
Chase Road	B3
Church Road	C1-C2-C3
Church Street	B2-C2-C1
College Road	C1
Depot Road	B2-C2
Downside	C1
Downs Road	C1
East Street	B2-B3-C3
East Way	A4
Felstead Road	B4
Gosfield Road	A2-A3

Grove Avenue	C2
Grove Road	C1-C2
Hamilton Close	A3-A4
Hawthorne Place	C2-C3
Hazon Way	B2-A2-A3-B3
Heathcote Road	B1
High Street	A2-B2
Hook Road	A4-B4-B3-B2
Horsley Close	A2-B2
Horton Hill	A4
Hurst Road	A4
Kendor Avenue	A4
Kiln Lane	C3-C4
Lintons Lane	C3
Long Mead Road	B4
Lower Court Road	A4
Manor Green Road	A4
Middle Lane	C3-C4
Miles Road	B3-B4-B3
Mill Road	C2-C3
Pikes Hill	C2
Pitt Road	C1
Pound Lane	A4-B4
Rosebank	A1
St Martins Avenue	C1
South Street	A1-A2
Station Approach	A2-B2
Stone's Road	C3-C4
Temple Road	A4-B4-A3-B3
The Grove	C1-C2
The Parade	B2-B1-C1
Upper Court Road	A4
Upper High Street	B2-C2
Victoria Place	C3
Waterloo Road	B2-B3
West Hill	A2
West Hill Avenue	A3
West Street	A1-A2
Wheelers Lane	A2
Woodcote Close	A1-B1-A1
Worple Road	B1-C1

Lambeth

Lambeth/Bermondsey A memory of other times for Lambeth can be found in Cherry Gardens Pier, which juts into the Thames at Bermondsey Wall East and recalls the days when this was a resort area (spa waters were found here in the 18th century). Some 13 Victorian churches can be found in the borough, and two places of interest are the Imperial War Museum and the Cuming Museum, which displays local archaeological finds. The Oval is the home of Surrey County Cricket Club.

Streatham Cinemas, dance halls, theatres, a bowling alley, an ice-rink and a swimming pool made Streatham a major entertainment centre for south London after the Second World War, and to some extent it still has that role. It first became popular with city merchants after the Great Fire because of its pleasant rural setting, and later on, spa waters were discovered on Streatham Common, which still has 36 acres of land.

Brixton The present site was a wasteland until suburban development reached it in the early 19th century. The large Italianate houses of St Johns Crescent are typical of the period.

Peckham was covered with market gardens and pasture until the 19th century. It still enjoys the 64 acres of Peckham Rye Common and the sports facilities of Peckham Rye Park. The house at No 2 Woods Road, Peckham, dates back to about 1690.

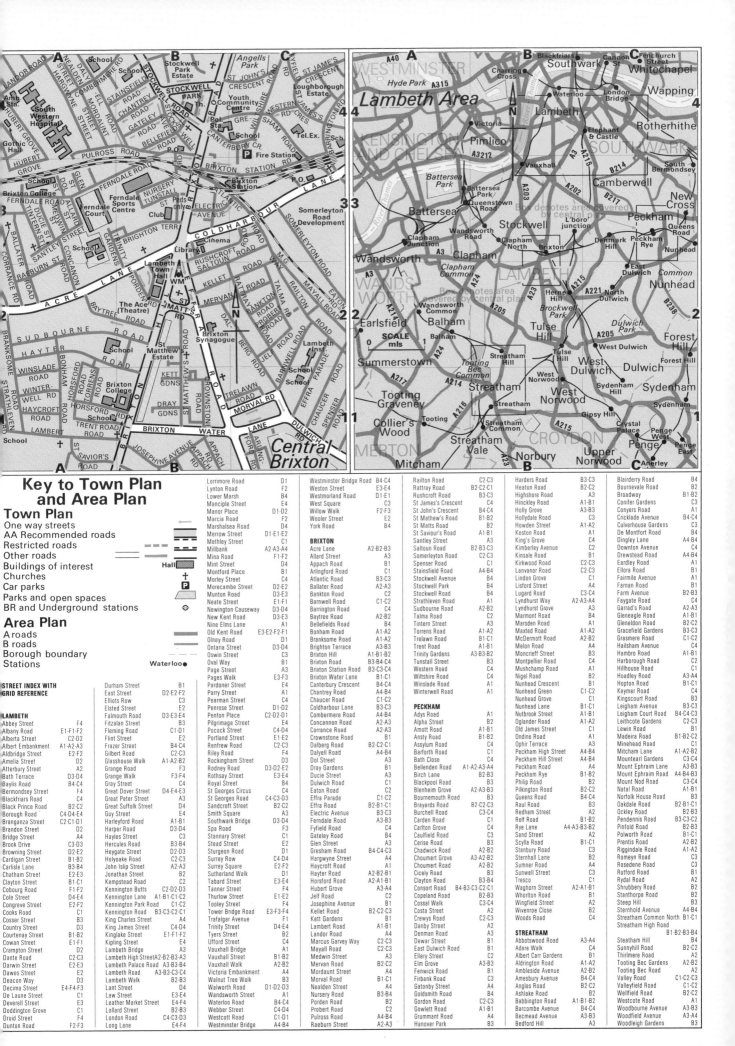

Key to Town Plan and Area Plan

Town Plan

One way streets
AA Recommended roads
Restricted roads
Other roads
Buildings of interest
Churches
Car parks
Parks and open spaces
BR and Underground stations

Area Plan

A roads
B roads
Borough boundary
Stations   Waterloo●

STREET INDEX WITH
GRID REFERENCE

LAMBETH

Abbey Street	F4
Albany Road	E1-F1-F2
Alberta Street	C2-D2
Albert Embankment	A1-A2-A3
Aldbridge Street	E2-F2
Amelia Street	D2
Atterbury Street	A2
Bath Terrace	D3-D4
Baylis Road	B4-C4
Bermondsey Street	F4
Blackfriars Road	C4
Black Prince Road	B2-C2
Branganza Street	C2-C1-D1
Brandon Street	D2
Bridge Street	A4
Brook Drive	C3-D3
Browning Street	D2-E2
Cardigan Street	B1-B2
Carlisle Lane	B3-B4
Chatham Street	E2-E3
Clayton Street	B1-C1
Cobourg Road	F1-F2
Cole Street	D4-E4
Congreve Street	E2-F2
Cooks Road	C1
Cosser Street	B3
Country Street	D3
Courtenay Street	B1-B2
Cowan Street	E1-F1
Crampton Street	D2
Dante Road	C2-C3
Darwin Street	E2-E3
Dawes Street	E2
Deacon Way	D3
Decima Street	E4-F4-F3
De Laune Street	C1
Deverell Street	E4
Doddington Grove	C1
Druid Street	F4
Dunton Road	F2-F3

Durham Street	B1
East Street	D2-E2-F2
Elliots Row	C3
Elsted Street	E2
Falmouth Road	D3-E3-E4
Fitzalan Street	B3
Fleming Road	C1-D1
Flint Street	E2
Frazer Street	B4-C4
Gilbert Road	C2-C3
Glasshouse Walk	A1-A2-B2
Grange Road	F3
Grange Walk	F3-F4
Gray Street	C4
Great Dover Street	D4-E4-E3
Great Peter Street	A3
Great Suffolk Street	D4
Guy Street	F4
Harleyford Road	A1-B1
Harper Road	D3-D4
Hayles Street	C3
Hercules Road	B3-B4
Heygate Street	D2-D3
Holyoake Road	C2-C3
John Islip Street	A2-A3
Jonathan Street	B2
Kempstead Road	C2
Kennington Butts	C2-D2-D3
Kennington Lane	A1-B1-C1-C2
Kennington Park Road	B3-C3-C2-C1
King Charles Street	A4
King James Street	C4
Kinglake Street	E1-F1-F2
Kipling Street	E4
Lambeth Bridge	A3
Lambeth High Street	A2-B2-B3-A3
Lambeth Palace Road	A3-B3-B4
Lambeth Road	A3-B3-C3-C4
Lambeth Walk	B2-B3
Lant Street	D4
Law Street	E3-E4
Leather Market Street	E4-F4
Lollard Street	B2-B3
London Road	C4-C3-D3
Long Lane	E4-F4

Lorrimore Road	D1
Lynton Road	F2
Lower Marsh	B4
Manciple Street	E4
Manor Place	D1-D2
Marcia Road	F2
Marshalsea Road	D4
Merrow Street	D1-E1-E2
Methley Street	C1
Millbank	A2-A3-A4
Mina Road	F1-F2
Mint Street	D4
Montford Place	B1
Morley Street	C4
Morecambe Street	D2-E2
Munton Road	D3-E3
Neate Street	E1-F1
Newington Causeway	D3-D4
New Kent Road	E1-E2
Nine Elms Lane	A1
Old Kent Road	E3-E2-F2-F1
Olney Road	D1
Ontario Street	D3-D4
Oswin Street	C3
Oval Way	B1
Page Street	A3
Pages Walk	E3-F3
Pardoner Street	E4
Parry Street	A1
Pearman Street	C4
Penrose Street	D1-D2
Penton Place	C2-D2-D1
Pilgrimage Street	E4
Pocock Street	C4-D4
Portland Street	E1-E2
Renfrew Road	C2-C3
Riley Road	F4
Rockingham Street	D3
Rodney Road	D3-D2-E2
Rothsay Street	E3-E4
Royal Street	B4
St Georges Circus	C4
St Georges Road	C4-C3-D3
Sandcroft Street	B2-C2
Smith Square	A3
Southwark Bridge	D3-D4
Spa Road	F3
Stannary Street	C1
Stead Street	E2
Sturgeon Road	D1
Surrey Row	C4-D4
Surrey Square	E2-F2
Sutherland Walk	D1
Tabard Street	E3-E4
Tanner Street	F4
Thurlow Street	E1-E2
Tooley Street	F4
Tower Bridge Road	E3-F3-F4
Trafalgar Avenue	F1
Trinity Street	D4-E4
Tyers Street	B2
Ufford Street	C4
Vauxhall Bridge	A1
Vauxhall Bridge	B1-B2
Vauxhall Walk	A2-B2
Victoria Embankment	A4
Walnut Tree Walk	B3
Walworth Road	D1-D2-D3
Wandsworth Street	A1
Waterloo Road	B4-C4
Webber Street	C4-D4
Westcott Road	C1-D1
Westminster Bridge	A4-B4

Westminster Bridge Road	B4-C4
Weston Street	E3-E4
Westmorland Road	D1-E1
West Square	C3
Willow Walk	F2-F3
Wooler Street	E2
York Road	B4

BRIXTON

Acre Lane	A2-B2-B3
Allard Street	A3
Appach Road	B1
Arlingford Road	C1
Atlantic Road	B3-C3
Ballater Road	A2-A3
Bankton Road	C2
Barnwell Road	C1-C2
Barrington Road	C4
Baytree Road	A2-B2
Bellefields Road	B4
Bonham Road	A1-A2
Branksome Road	A1-A2
Brighton Terrace	A3-B3
Brixton Hill	A1-B1-B2
Brixton Road	B3-B4-C4
Brixton Station Road	B3-C3-C4
Brixton Water Lane	B1-C1
Canterbury Crescent	B4-C4
Chantry Road	A4-B4
Chaucer Road	C1-C2
Coldharbour Lane	B3-C3
Combermere Road	A4-B4
Concannon Road	A2-A3
Corrance Road	A2-A3
Crownstone Road	B1
Dalberg Road	B2-C2-C1
Dalyell Road	A4-B4
Dol Street	A4
Dray Gardens	B1
Ducie Street	B2
Dulwich Road	C1
Eaton Road	C2
Effra Parade	C1-C2
Effra Road	B2-B1-C1
Electric Avenue	B3-C3
Ferndale Road	A3-B3
Fyfield Road	C2
Gateley Road	B4
Glen Street	A4
Gresham Road	B4-C4-C3
Hargwyne Street	A4
Haycroft Road	A1
Hayter Road	A2-B2-B1
Horsford Road	A2-A1-B1
Hubert Grove	A3-A4
Jelf Road	C2
Josephine Avenue	B1
Kellet Road	B2-C2-C3
Kett Gardens	B1
Lambert Road	A1-B1
Landor Road	A4
Marcus Garvey Way	C2-C3
Mayall Road	C2-C3
Medwin Street	A3
Mervan Road	B2-C2
Mordaunt Street	A4
Morval Road	C2
Nealden Street	A4
Nursery Road	B3-B4
Porden Road	B2
Probert Road	C2
Pulross Road	A4-B4
Raeburn Street	A2-A3

Railton Road	C2-C3
Rattray Road	B2-C2-C1
Rushcroft Road	B3-C3
St James's Crescent	C4
St John's Crescent	B4-C4
St Mathew's Road	B1-B2
St Matts Road	B2
St Saviour's Road	A1-B1
Santley Street	A3
Saltoun Road	B2-B3-C3
Somerleyton Road	C2-C3
Spenser Road	C1
Stainsfield Road	A4-B4
Stockwell Avenue	B4
Stockwell Park	B4
Stockwell Road	B4
Strathleven Road	A1
Sudbourne Road	A2-B2
Talma Road	C2
Tintern Street	A3
Torrens Road	A1-A2
Trelawn Road	B1-C1
Trent Road	A1-B1
Trinity Gardens	A3-B3-B2
Tunstall Road	B3
Western Road	C4
Wiltshire Road	C4
Winslade Road	A1
Winterwell Road	A1

PECKHAM

Adys Road	A1
Alpha Street	B2
Amott Road	A1-B1
Ansty Road	B1-B2
Assylum Road	C4
Barforth Road	C1
Bath Close	C4
Bellenden Road	A1-A2-A3-A4
Birch Lane	B2-B3
Blackpool Road	B3
Blenheim Grove	A2-A3-B3
Bournemouth Road	B3
Brayards Road	B2-C2-C3
Burchell Road	C3-C4
Carden Road	C1
Carlton Grove	C4
Caulfield Road	C4
Cerise Road	B3
Chadwick Road	A2-B2
Choumert Grove	A3-A2-B2
Choumert Road	A2-B2
Cicely Road	B3
Clayton Road	B3-B4
Consort Road	B4-B3-C3-C2-C1
Copeland Road	B2-B3
Cossal Walk	C3-C4
Costa Street	A2
Crewys Road	C2-C3
Danby Street	A2
Denman Road	A3
Dewar Street	B1
East Dulwich Road	B1
Ellery Street	C2
Elm Grove	A3-B3
Fenwick Road	B1
Firbank Road	B2
Gatonby Street	A4
Goldsmith Road	B4
Gordon Road	C2-C3
Gowlett Road	A1-B1
Grummant Road	A4
Hanover Park	B3

Harders Road	B3-C3
Heaton Road	B2-C2
Highshore Road	A3
Hinckley Road	A1-B1
Holly Grove	A3-B3
Hollydale Road	C3
Howden Road	A1-A2
Keston Road	A1
King's Grove	C4
Kimberley Avenue	C2
Kinsale Road	B1
Kirkwood Road	C2-C3
Lanvanor Road	C2-C3
Lindon Grove	C1
Lisford Street	A4
Lugard Road	C3-C4
Lyndhurst Way	A2-A3-A4
Lyndhurst Grove	A3
Marmont Road	B4
Marsden Road	A1
Maxted Road	A1-A2
McDermott Road	A2-B2
Melon Road	A3
Moncrieff Street	B3
Montpellier Road	C4
Mushchamp Road	A1
Nigel Road	B2
Nunhead Crescent	B1
Nunhead Green	C1-C2
Nunhead Grove	C1
Nunhead Lane	B1-C1
Nutbrook Street	A1-B1
Oglander Road	A1-A2
Old James Street	C1
Ondine Road	A1
Ophir Terrace	A3
Peckham High Street	A4-B4
Peckham Hill Street	A4-B4
Peckham Road	A4
Peckham Rye	B1-B2
Philip Road	B2
Pilkington Road	B2-C2
Queens Road	B4-C4
Raul Road	B3
Redham Street	A2
Relf Road	B1-B2
Rye Lane	A4-A3-B3-B2
Sand Street	A2
Scylla Road	B1-C1
Stanbury Road	C3
Sternhall Lane	B2
Sumner Road	A4
Sunwell Street	C3
Tresco	C1
Waghorn Street	A2-A1-B1
Whorlton Road	B1
Wingfield Street	A2
Wivenroe Close	B2
Woods Road	C4

STREATHAM

Abbotswood Road	A3-A4
Adare Walk	A4
Albert Carr Gardens	B1
Aldrington Road	A1-A2
Ambleside Avenue	A2-B2
Amesbury Avenue	B4-C4
Angles Road	B2-C2
Ashlake Road	B2
Babbington Road	A1-B1-B2
Barcombe Avenue	B4-C4
Becmead Avenue	A3-B3
Bedford Hill	A3

Blairderry Road	B4
Bournevale Road	B2
Broadway	B1-B2
Conifer Gardens	C3
Conyers Road	A1
Cricklade Avenue	B4-C4
Culverhouse Gardens	C3
De Montfort Road	A4-B4
Dingley Lane	A4-B4
Downton Avenue	C4
Drewstead Road	A4-B4
Eardley Road	A1
Ellora Road	B1
Fairmile Avenue	A1
Farnan Road	B1
Farm Avenue	B2-B3
Faygate Road	C4
Garrad's Road	A2-A3
Gleneagle Road	A1-B1
Gleneldon Road	B2-C2
Gracefield Gardens	B3-C3
Grasmere Road	C1-C2
Hailsham Avenue	C4
Hambro Road	A1-B1
Harborough Road	C2
Hillhouse Road	C1
Hoadley Road	A3-A4
Hopton Road	B1-C1
Keymer Road	C4
Kingscourt Road	B3
Leigham Avenue	B3-C3
Leigham Court Road	B4-C4-C3
Leithcote Gardens	C2-C3
Lewin Road	B1
Madeira Road	B1-B2-C2
Minehead Road	C3
Mitcham Lane	A1-A2-B2
Mount Ephraim Lane	A3-B3
Mount Ephraim Road	A4-B4-B3
Mount Nod Road	C3-C4
Natal Road	A1-B1
Norfolk House Road	B3
Oakdale Road	B2-B1-C1
Ockley Road	B2-B3
Pendennis Road	B3-C3-C2
Pinfold Road	B2-B3
Polworth Road	B1-C1
Prentis Road	A2-B2
Riggindale Road	A1-A2
Romeyn Road	C3
Rosedene Road	C3
Rutford Road	B1
Rydal Road	A2
Shrubbery Road	B2
Stanthorpe Road	B2
Steep Hill	B3
Sternhold Avenue	A4-B4
Streatham Common North	B1-C1
Streatham High Road	B1-B2-B3-B4
Steatham Hill	B4
Sunnyhill Road	B2-B3
Thirlmere Road	A2
Tooting Bec Gardens	A2-B2
Tooting Bec Road	A2
Valley Road	C1-C2-C3
Valleyfield Road	C1-C2
Wellfield Road	B2-C2
Westcote Road	A1
Woodbourne Avenue	A3-B3
Woodfield Avenue	A3-A4
Woodleigh Gardens	B3

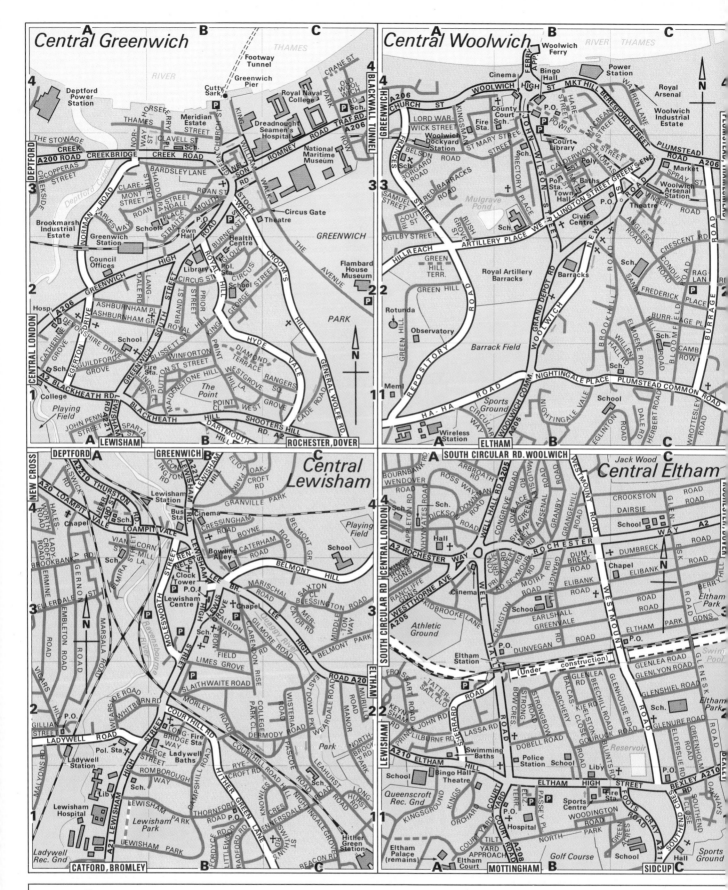

Lewisham

This is a popular destination for south-east Londoners, who come for the good shopping and leisure facilities. Most of these can be found in the Riverside Centre, which also offers the sports facilities of the Lewisham Leisure Centre, and, for social functions, the Riverdale Hall.

Greenwich lies at the heart of Britain's maritime traditions. The Royal Naval College and the National Maritime Museum provide a fascinating insight into the seafaring past. Open to visitors on Greenwich pier is Gypsy Moth IV, the boat in which Sir Francis Chichester sailed singlehanded round the world in 1966. Cutty Sark, a 19th-century clipper, is in dry dock nearby.

The Greenwich Meridian, source of Greenwich Mean Time, can be seen outside the Old Royal Observatory (now a museum) which stands in the extensive and beautiful grounds of Greenwich Park.

The Greenwich Festival takes place each June at various venues throughout the Borough, and offers some 200 events featuring international artists.

Woolwich The South-East London Aquatic Centre, in the Dockyard, offers facilities for most water sports. The Rotunda houses the Museum of Artillery.

Eltham is notable as the birthplace of Bob Hope — and for the restored 14th-century Eltham Palace. The Great Hall was built originally by Edward IV, during the 15th century.

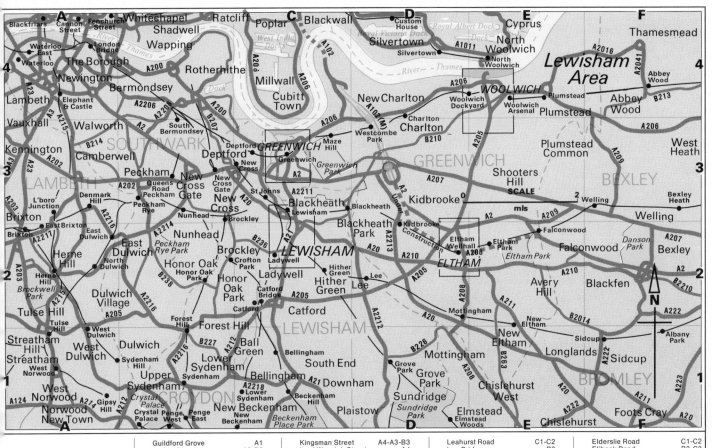

LEGEND

Town Plan

AA recommended route
Restricted roads
Other roads
Buildings of interest   P.O.
Car parks   P
Parks and open spaces
One way streets

Area Plan

A roads
B roads
Stations   Vauxhall

Street Index with Grid Reference

Greenwich

Ashburnham Grove	A2-B2
Ashburnham Place	A2-B2
Bardsley Lane	A3-B3
Blackheath Hill	A1-B1
Blackheath Road	A1
Blissett Street	A1-B1-B2
Brand Street	B2
Burney Street	B2-B3
Cade Road	C1
Catherine Grove	A1-A2
Circus Street	B2
Claremont Street	B3-A3
Clavell Street	A3
Copperas Street	A3
Crane Street	C4
Creek Bridge	A3
Creek Road	A3-B3
Creekside	A3
Croom's Hill	B3-B2-C2-C1
Dartmouth Hill	B1
Devonshire Drive	A1-A2
Diamond Terrace	B1-C1
Dutton Street	B1
Egerton Drive	A1-A2
General Wolfe Road	C1
Gloucester Circus	B2
Greenwich Church Street	B3-B4
Greenwich High Road	A2-B2-B3
Greenwich South Street	A1-B1-B2
Guildford Grove	A1
Haddo Street	A3-B3
Horseferry Place	A4-B4-B3
Hyde Vale	B2-B1-C1
John Penn Street	A1
King George Street	B2-C2
King William Walk	B4-B3-C3
Langdale Road	A2
Lewisham Road	A1
Lindsell Street	A1-B1
Maidstone Hill	B1
Nelson Road	B3
Norman Road	A2-A3
Norway Street	A3-A4
Old Woolwich Road	C4
Park Row	C3-C4
Point Close	B1
Point Hill	B1-B2
Prior Street	B2
Randall Place	B3
Rangers Square	C1
Romney Road	B3-C3-C4
Roan Street	A3-B3
Royal Hill	B2
Shooters Hill Road	B1-C1
Sparta Street	A1
Stockwell Street	B3
Straits Mouth	B3-B2
Tarves Way	A3
Thames Street	A4-B4-B3
The Avenue	C2-C3
The Stowage	A3
Trafalgar Road	C4
West Grove	B1-C1
Westgrove Lane	B1
Winforton Street	B1

Woolwich

Anglesea Road	C2-C3
Artillery Place	A2-B2-B3
Belson Road	A3
Beresford Street	B4-C4-C3
Bloomfield Road	C1-C2
Borgard Road	A3
Brookhill Road	B1-B2-C2-C3
Burrage Place	C2
Burrage Road	C1-C2-C3
Calderwood Street	B3
Cambridge Row	C1
Church Street	A4
Circular Way	A1
Conduit Road	C2
Crescent Road	C2
Dale Road	C2
Eglinton Road	B1-C1
Elmdene Road	C1-C2
Ferry Approach	B4
Frances Street	A2-A3-A4
Frederick Place	C2
Grand Depot Road	B2
Green Hill	A1-A2
Green Hill Terrace	A2
Green's End	C3
Ha-Ha Road	A1-B1
Hare Street	B4
Herbert Road	A2
Hill Reach	A2
John Wilson Street	B2-B3-B4

Kingsman Street	A4-A3-B3
Lord Warwick Street	A4
Macbean Street	B3-B4-C4
Market Hill	B4
Market Street	B3
Nightingale Place	B1
Nightingale Vale	B1
Ogilby Street	A3
Plumstead Common Road	C1
Plumstead Road	C4
Powis Street	B4-B3-C3
Rectory Place	B3
Repository Road	A1-A2
Ridout Street	A3
Rush Grove Street	A2-A3
St Mary Street	A3-A4-B4
Samuel Street	A3
Sandy Hill Road	C1-C2
Spray Street	C3
Thomas Street	B3-C3
Vincent Road	C2
Warren Lane	B4-C4-C3
Wellington Street	B3
Willenhall Road	B2-C2-C1
Woolwich Common	B1
Woolwich High Street	A4-B4
Woolwich New Road	B1-B2-B3-C3
Wrottesley Road	C1

Lewisham

Albion Way	B3
Algernon Road	A2-A3-A4
Beacon Road	C1
Belmont Grove	C3-C4
Belmont Hill	B3-C3
Belmont Park	C3
Blessington Road	C3
Bonfield Road	B3-C3
Boyne Road	B4-C4-C3
Brookbank Road	A3
Campshill Road	B1-B2
Caterham Road	B4-C4
Clarendon Rise	B2-B3
College Park Close	B2
Connington Road	B4
Cornmill Lane	A4
Courthill Road	B2-B1-C1
Cressingham Road	B4
Dermody Road	B2-C2
Eastdown Park	C2
Eliot Park	B4
Ellerdale Street	A3
Elmira Street	A3-A4
Elswick Road	A4
Embleton Road	A2-A3
Ennersdale Road	B1-C1
Ermine Road	A2-A3
Fordyce Road	A2
Gillian Street	A2
Gilmore Road	B3-C3-C2
Granville Park	B4-C4
Halesworth Road	A4
Hither Green Lane	B2-B1-C1
Jerrard Street	A4
Knowles Hill Crescent	C1
Ladycroft Road	A3-A4
Ladywell Road	A2

Leahurst Road	C1-C2
Lee Bridge	B3
Lee High Road	B3-C3-C2
Legge Street	A2-B2
Lewis Grove	B3
Lewisham High Street	A1-A2-B2-B3-B4
Lewisham Hill	B3
Lewisham Park	A1-B1
Lewisham Road	B4
Limes Grove	B2
Littlewood Road	B1
Loampit Vale	A4-B4
Longbridge Way	B2
Longhurst Road	C1
Malyons Road	A1-A2
Manor Park	C1-C2
Marischal Road	B3-C3
Marsala Road	A2-A3
Mercator Road	C3
Middleton Way	C3
Molesworth Street	B3-B4
Morley Road	B2
Murillo Road	C2
Nightingale Grove	C1
Northbrook Road	C2
Oakcroft Road	B4-C4
Pascoe Road	C1-C2
Radford Road	B1
Rennel Street	B3-B4
Romborough Way	A1-B1
Ryecroft Road	B1
St Swithun's Road	C1
Saxton Close	C3
Slaithwaite Road	B2
Thornford Road	B1
Thurston Road	A4
Vian Street	A4
Vicars Hill	A2
Weardale Road	C2
Wearside Road	A2
Whitburn Road	A2-B2
Wisteria Road	C2

Eltham

Admiral Seymour Road	A3-B3-B4
Appleton Road	A4
Arbroath Road	A4-B4
Archery Road	B1-B2
Arsenal Road	B4
Balcaskie Road	B2
Beechill Road	B2
Berryhill	C3
Bexley Road	C1-C2
Blunts Road	B1-B2
Bournbank Road	A4
Congreve Road	B3-B4
Court Road	A1-B1
Court Yard	A1-B1
Craigton Road	B3
Crookston Road	B4-C4
Dairsie Road	B4-C4
Dickson Road	A4
Dobell Road	B2
Downman Road	A4
Dumbreck Road	B3-C3-C4
Dunvegan Road	B3-C3
Earlshall Road	B3-C3

Elderslie Road	C1-C2
Elibank Road	B3-C3
Elizabeth Terrace	B1
Elston Close	B3
Eltham High Street	B1-C1
Eltham Hill	A2-A1-B1
Eltham Park Gardens	C3
Foots Cray Road	C1
Froissart Road	A2
Glenesk Road	C2-C3-C4
Glenhouse Road	B2-C2
Glenlea Road	B2-C2-C3
Glenlyon Road	C2
Glenshiel Road	C2
Glenure Road	C2
Gourock Road	B2-C2
Granby Road	B4
Grangehill Road	B3-B4
Green Acres	B1-C1
Greenholm Road	C1-C2
Greenvale Road	B3-C3
Keynsham Road	A2
Kidbrooke Lane	A3
Kingsground	A1
Kingsholm Gardens	A3-A4
Kings Orchard	A1
Lassa Road	A2-B2
Lilburne Road	A2
Lovelace Green	B4
Maudsley Road	B4
Moira Road	B3-B4
North Park	B1-C1
Oakways	C1
Passey Place	B1
Prince John Road	A2
Prince Rupert Road	A3-B3-B4
Rancliffe Gardens	B4
Rochester Way	A4-A3-A4-B4-C4
Ross Way	A2
Sherrard Road	A2-B2
Shrapnel Road	B4
Southend Close	C1
Southend Crescent	C1
Strongbow Crescent	B2
Strongbow Road	B2
Tattersall Close	A2
Tilt Yard Approach	A1-B1
Wendover Road	B4
Well Hall Road	B1-B2-B3-A3-A4-B4
Westhorne Avenue	A3
Westmount Road	B4-B3-C3-C2-C1
Whynates Road	A4
Woodington Road	B1-C1

Richmond

Red deer and fallow deer roam Richmond Park's 2,500 acres of woodland and common, and Richmond itself has kept a village-like atmosphere in spite of a great deal of development over the last two centuries. Around the Green, antique and curio shops can be found nestling among the narrow lanes and alleyways of a bygone age. Richmond's other great attraction is the river: this has been a fashionable residential area for several hundred years, due to its pleasant Thames-side location and its proximity to Hampton Court Palace.

Twickenham Regular international matches are played during the season at this home of Rugby Union Football. Places of interest include Marble Hill House, a Palladian villa set in pleasant parkland, the Orleans House Gallery, which has paintings of local scenes, and the nearby Royal Botanic Gardens at Kew.

Hounslow Gunpowder and swords were the pride of Hounslow in the 17th century; three hundred years later, the area is mainly residential, with good shopping and leisure facilities.

Brentford's modern urban appearance belies its numerous places of interest. Gunnersbury Park has a local history museum, and St George's Church, in the High Street, houses a collection of musical instruments. A museum of steam engines can be seen at Kew Bridge Pumping Station.

34

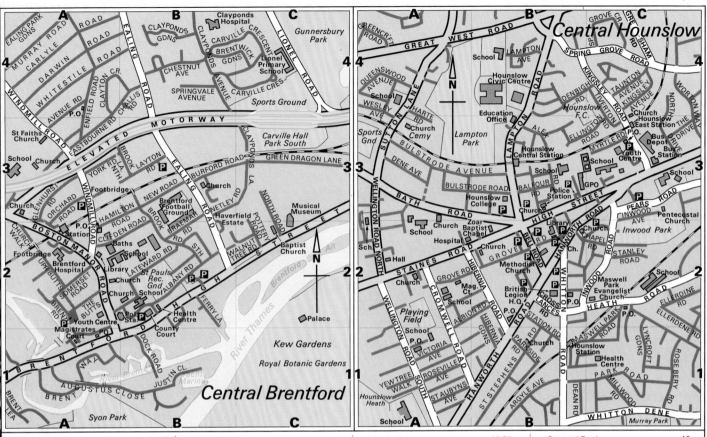

Key to Town Plan and Area Plan

Town Plan

AA Recommended roads	
Other roads	
Restricted roads	
Buildings of interest	
Churches	Church
Car Parks	P
Parks and open spaces	
AA Service Centre	AA

Area Plan

A roads	
B roads	
Locations	Honley O
Urban area	

Richmond

Albert Road	C2-C3
Alton Road	C3
Audley Road	C2
Avalon Terrace	C3-C4
Beaumont Avenue	C4
Bridge Street	A1-A2
Cambridge Road	A1
Cardigan Road	B1
Castle Gate	C4
Cedar Terrace	C4
Chester Avenue	C1
Chislehurst Road	B1
Church Road	B3-B2-C2-C1
Clevedon Road	A1
Cresswell Road	A1
Crofton Terrace	C4
Dunstable Road	B3-C3
Dynevor Road	B2
Ellerker Gardens	B1
Eton Street	B2-B3
Evelyn Road	B4
Friars Lane	A2
Friars Stile Road	B1-C1
George Street	A2-A3
Greenside	A2-A3
Grosvenor Road	B2
Halford Road	B2
Hill Street	A2
Houblon Road	C2-C3
Jocelyn Road	B4-C4
Kew Foot Road	B4
Kew Road	B3-B4-C4
Kings Road	C1-C2-C3
Lancaster Park	B1-B2
Larkfield Road	B3-C3
Lower Mortlake Road	B4-C4
Maid of Honour Road	A3-A2
Marchmont Road	C1-C2
Marlborough Road	C1
Montague Road	B1
Mount Ararat Road	B2-B1-C1
Onslow Avenue	B1-B2
Onslow Road	B1-C1

Pagoda Avenue	C4
Paradise Road	B2
Park Hill	C1
Park Lane	A3-B3
Park Road	C1
Parkshot	A3-B3-B4
Pembroke Villas	A3
Petersham Road	A2-A1-B1
Portland Terrace	A3
Princes Road	C2-C3
Queens Rise	C1
Queens Road	C1
Red Lion Street	A2-B2
Richmond Hill	A1-B1
Richmond Road	A1
Royston Road	B2-C2
Selwyn Avenue	C4
Sheendale Road	C4
Sheen Park	C3
Sheen Road	B3-B2-B3-C3
Sheen Vale	C4
Spring Grove Road	C2
Sydney Road	B3
The Hermitage	A2-B2
The Orange Tree	A4-B4
The Quadrant	A3-B3
The Vineyard	A1-B1-B2
Townshend Road	C3
Townshend Terrace	C3
Twickenham Road	A3-A4
Water Lane	A2
Worple Way	C3

Twickenham

Amyand Park Road	C3-C4
Arragon Road	C2
Bell Lane	C2
Chertsey Road	A3-A4-B3-B4-C4
Chudleigh Road	A3-B3
Chuch Street	C2
Clifden Road	B2
Cole Park Road	B3-C3-B3-B4
Colne Road	A1-A2
Copthall Gardens	B2
Court Way	A3-B3
Craneford Way	A2-A3-B3
Cross Deep	B1-B2
Edwin Road	A2
Egerton Road	A3
Erncroft Way	B3-B4
Fulwood Gardens	B4
Glebeside	B4
Godstone Road	C3-C4
Gould Road	A2
Grange Avenue	A1
Grosvenor Road	B2
Grotto Road	B1
Grove Avenue	B2
Hampton Road	A1
Heathfield North	A3-B3
Heathfield South	A3-B3
Heath Gardens	A1-B1
Heath Road	A1-A2-B2
Hill View Road	B4-C4
Holly Road	B2
Holmes Road	B1
Kenley Road	C4
King Street	B2-C2
Latham Road	B3
Laurel Avenue	A2-B2
Lebanon Park	C2
Lime Grove	B3

Lion Road	A2-B2
London Road	B4-B3-B2-C2
Marble Hill Gardens	C3
Marlow Crescent	B4
May Road	A1-A2
Oak Lane	C2-C3
Orchard Road	C4
Popes Avenue	A1
Popes Grove	A1-B1
Queens Road	B2
Radnor Road	B1-B2
Richmond Road	C2-C3
Rugby Road	A4
St Margaret's Road	C4
Saville Road	B1
Sherland Road	B2
Sidney Road	C4
Sion Road	C2
Station Road	B2
Strafford Road	C2-C3
The Avenue	C4
The Embankment	C1-C2
The Green	A1
Upper Grotto Road	A1-B1
Walpole Road	A1
Whitton Road	A3-A4-A3-B3
York Street	C2

Brentford

Albany Road	B2
Augustus Close	A1-B1
Avenue Road	A3-A4
Boston Manor Road	A1-A2-A3
Braemar Road	B2-B3
Brentford High Street	A1-B1-B2-C2-C3
Brent Lea	A1
Brent Road	A2
Brent Way	A1
Brentwick Gardens	B4-C4
Brook Lane North	A3-B3
Brook Road South	B2-B3
Burford Road	B3-C3
Carlyle Road	B2
Carville Crescent	B4-C4-B4
Challis Road	A4-B4
Chestnut Avenue	B4
Church Walk	A2
Clayponds Avenue	B4
Clayponds Gardens	B4
Clayponds Lane	C3
Clayton Crescent	A4-B4
Clifden Road	A2-B2-B3
Darwin Road	A4-B4
Dock Road	B1
Ealing Park Gardens	A4
Ealing Road	B4-B3-B2
Eastbourne Road	A3-A4
Enfield Road	A3-A4
Ferry Lane	B2
Glenhurst Road	A2-A3
Green Dragon Lane	C3
Hamilton Road	A2-A3-B3
Justin Close	B1
Lateward Road	B2
Layton Road	B3
Lionel Road	C4
Murray Road	A4
Netley Road	B3-C3
New Road	B3
North Road	C2-C3
Orchard Road	A2-A3
Pottery Road	C2-C3

Somerset Road	A2
Springvale Avenue	B4
The Butts	A2
Upper Butts	A2
Walnut Tree Road	B2-C2
Windmill Road	A2-A3-A4
Whitstile Road	A4-B4
York Road	A3

Hounslow

Albion Road	A1-A2-B2
Alexandra Road	B3
Argyle Avenue	B1
Balfour Road	B3
Bath Road	A3-B3-B2
Bell Road	B2
Bulstrode Avenue	A3-B3
Bulstrode Road	A3-B3
Chapel Road	B2-C2
Cromwell Road	A2-A1-B1
Cross Lances Road	B2
Dean Road	B1
Denbigh Road	B4-C4-B2
Dene Avenue	A3
Ellerdine Road	C1-C2
Ellington Road	B3-C3
Great West Road	A4-B4
Greencroft Road	A4
Gresham Road	C4
Grove Road	A2-B2
Hanworth Road	A1-B1-B2-B3-C2-C3
Harte Road	A3-A4
Heath Road	B2-C2
Hibernia Gardens	B1-B2
Hibernia Road	A2-B2-B1
High Street	B2-B3-C3
Inwood Avenue	C2-C3
Inwood Road	B2-C2-C3
Kingsley Avenue	C4
Kingsley Road	B4-C4-C3
Lampton Avenue	B4
Lampton Road	B3-B4
Lyncroft Gardens	C1-C2
Maswell Park Road	B1-C1-C2
Millwood Road	C1
Myrtle Road	C3
North Drive	C3-C4
Park Road	B1-C1
Parkside Road	B1
Pears Road	C3
Queensway Avenue	A4
Rosebery Road	C1
Roseville Road	A1
St Aubyns Avenue	A1
St Stephens Road	B1
Spring Grove Crescent	C4
Spring Grove Road	B4-C4
Staines Road	A2
Stanley Road	C2
Station Road	B1-B2
Sutton Lane	A3-A4
Taunton Avenue	C4
The Drive	C3
Tiverton Road	C3-C4
Victoria Avenue	A1
Wellington Road North	A2-A3
Wellington Road South	A1-A2
Wesley Avenue	A3-A4
Whitton Dene	B1-C1
Whitton Road	B1-B2
Worton Way	C3-C4
Yew Tree Walk	A1

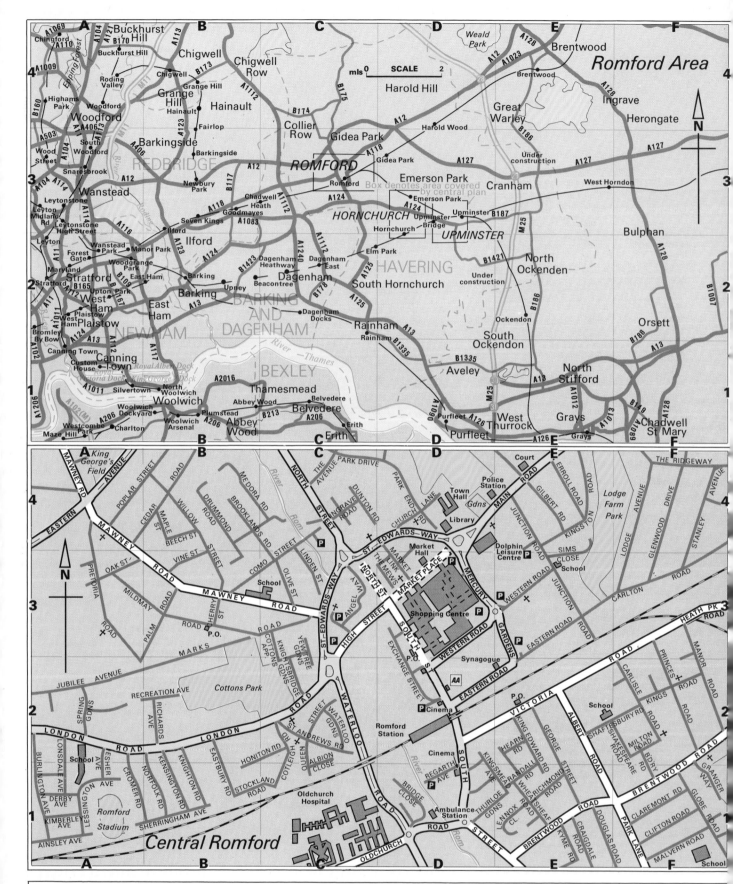

Romford

Reputed to have some of the finest shopping facilities on the east side of London, Romford mixes the ancient with the modern in its high streets and traffic areas. Centrepiece of all shopping is Romford Market, where traders have been setting up stall three times a week for the past 700 years.

The oldest-founded building still standing in Romford is thought to be St Edward's Church, which was rebuilt in 1850 and has some interesting monuments. The Golden Lion survives as a fine example of an old coaching inn.

Hornchurch A bull's head and horns hung over the east window of St Andrew's Church gave Hornchurch its name — thought to be the only example in the country to be used instead of the traditional east end cross. Also unique to the church is the tomb of Thomas Witherings,

17th-century organiser of the postal system.

Modern shops line the High Street, which was once known as Pelt Street: Hornchurch was famous for its leather goods in the 13th century. The Queens Theatre stages concerts and professional repertory performances of a high standard.

Upminster's windmill was constructed in 1803 and has remained in excellent condition. Other buildings of interest include Upminster Hall and 15th-century Upminster Tithe Barn.

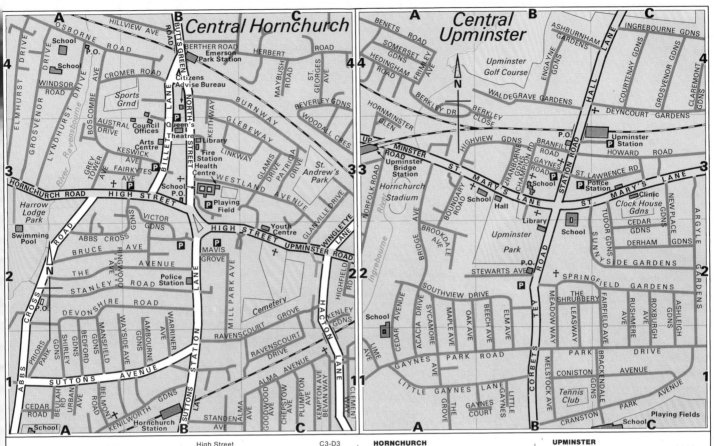

LEGEND

Town Plan

AA Recommended roads	
Other roads	
Restricted roads	
Buildings of interest	Cinema
Car Parks	P
Parks and open spaces	

Area Plan

A roads	
B roads	
Stations	Forest Bridge ●
Borough Boundary	

STREET INDEX WITH GRID REFERENCE

ROMFORD

Ainsley Avenue	A1
Albert Road	E1-E2
Albion Close	C1-C2
Angel Way	C3
Beech Street	B4
Boundary Road	F1-F2
Brentwood Road	E1-F1-F2
Bridge Close	D1
Brooklands Road	B4-C4-C3
Burlington Avenue	A1-A2
Carlisle Road	F2
Carlton Road	E3-F3-F4
Cedar Road	A4-B4
Cherry Street	B3
Church Lane	D4
Claremont Road	F1
Clifton Road	F1
Como Street	B3-C3-C4
Cotleigh Road	C1-C2
Cottons Approach	C2-C3
Craigdale Road	E1
Cromer Road	A2-A1-B1
Derby Avenue	A1
Douglas Road	E1-F1
Drummond Road	B3-B4
Dunton Road	C4
Eastbury Road	B1-B2
Eastern Avenue	A4
Eastern Road	D2-E2-E3
Erroll Road	E4
Esher Avenue	A1-A2
Exchange Street	E1-E2
George Street	E1-E2
Gilbert Road	E4
Glenwood Drive	F3-F4
Globe Road	F1
Granger Way	F1-F2
Hearn Road	E2
Heath Park Road	F3

High Street	C3-D3
Honiton Road	B1-B2-C2
Ingrave Road	C4
Jubilee Avenue	A2
Junction Road	E3-E4
Kensington Road	B1-B2
Kimberley Avenue	A1
King Edward Road	E1-E2
Kings Road	F2
Kingsmead Avenue	D2-D1-E1
Kingston Road	E4
Knighton Road	B1-B2
Knightsbridge Gardens	C2-C3
Kyme Road	E1
Lennox Close	E1
Lessington Avenue	A1
Linden Street	C3-C4
Lodge Avenue	F3-F4
London Road	A2-B2-C2
Lonsdale Avenue	A1-A2
Main Road	D4-E4
Malvern Road	F1
Manor Road	F2-F3
Maple Street	B4
Market Link	D3-D4
Market Place	D3
Marks Road	B2-B3-C3
Mawney Road	A4-A3-B3-C3
Medora Road	B4-C4
Mercury Gardens	D3-E3
Mildmay Road	A3-B3
Milton Road	F2
Norfolk Road	B1-B2
North Street	C4-C3-D3
Oak Street	A3
Oldchurch Road	C1-D1
Olive Street	C3
Palm Road	A3-B3
Park Drive	C4-D4
Park Lane	F1
Park End Road	D4
Pretoria Road	A2-A3-A4
Princes Road	F2-F3
Poplar Street	A4-B4
Queen Street	C1-C2
Randall Road	E1-E2
Recreation Avenue	A2-B2
Regarth Avenue	D1
Richards Avenue	B2
Richmond Road	E1
St Andrews Road	C2
St Edwards Way	C2-C3-C4-D4
Shaftesbury Road	E2-F2
Shakespeare Road	E2-F2
Sherringham Avenue	A1-B1
Sims Close	E3-E4
South Street	D3-D2-D1-E1
Spring Gardens	A2
Stanley Avenue	F3-F4
Stockland Road	B1-C1
The Avenue	C4
The Mews	D3
The Ridgeway	F4
Thurloe Gardens	D1-E1
Victoria Road	D2-E2-E3-F3
Vine Street	B3
Waterloo Gardens	C2
Waterloo Road	C2-C1-D1
Western Road	D2-D3-E3
Wheatsheaf Road	E1
Willow Street	B3-B4
Yew Tree Gardens	C2-C3

HORNCHURCH

Abbs Cross Gardens	A2-B2-C2
Abbs Cross Road	A1-A2-A3
Alma Avenue	A3
Austral Drive	A3
Bedford Gardens	A1-A2
Belmont Road	A1
Berther Road	B4
Beulah Road	A1
Bevan Way	C1
Beverley Gardens	C4
Billet Lane	B3-B4
Boscombe Avenue	A3-A4
Bruce Avenue	A2-B2
Burnway	B4-C4-C3
Butts Green Road	B4
Cedar Road	A1
Chepstow Avenue	C1
Clement Way	C1
Cromer Road	A4-B4
Devonshire Road	A2-B2
Elmhurst Drive	A3-A4
Fairkytes Avenue	A3-B3
Glamis Drive	C3
Glanville Drive	C2-C3
Glebeway	B4-B3-C3
Grey Tower Avenue	A3
Goodwood Avenue	C1
Grosvenor Drive	A3-A4
Hacton Lane	C1-C2
Herbert Road	C4
High Street	A3-B3-B2-C2
Highfield Road	C2
Hillview Avenue	A4-B4
Hornchurch Road	A3
Keithway	B3-B4
Kempton Avenue	C1
Kenilworth Gardens	A1-B1
Kenley Gardens	C2
Keswick Avenue	A3-B3
Lambourne Gardens	B1-B2
Linkway	B3-C3
Lyndhurst Drive	A3-A4
Mansfield Gardens	A1-A2
Mavis Grove	B2
Maybush Road	C4
Mill Park Avenue	B1-B2
North Street	B3-B4
Osborne Road	A4-B4
Patricia Drive	C3
Plumpton Avenue	C1
Priors Park	A1
Ravenscourt Drive	C1
Ravenscourt Grove	B1-C1-C2
Ringwood Avenue	A2
St Georges Avenue	C4
Shirley Gardens	A1-C1
Standen Avenue	B1-C1
Stanley Road	A2-B2
Station Lane	B1-B2
Suttons Avenue	A1-B1
Suttons Lane	B1
The Avenue	A2-B2
Upminster Road	C2
Urban Avenue	A1
Victor Gardens	B2-B3
Warriner Avenue	B1-B2
Wayside Avenue	A1-A2-B1
Westland Avenue	B3-C3-C2
Windsor Road	A4
Wingletye Lane	C2-C3
Woodall Crescent	C3

UPMINSTER

Acacia Drive	A1-A2
Argyle Gardens	C1-C2-C3
Ashburnham Gardens	B4-C4
Ashleigh Gardens	C1-C2
Beech Avenue	B1-B2
Benets Road	A4
Berkley Close	A4-B4-B5
Berkley Drive	A4-A3
Boundary Road	A2-A3
Brackendale Gardens	C1
Branfill Road	B3
Bridge Avenue	A2-A3
Brookdale Avenue	A2
Cedar Avenue	A1-A2
Cedar Gardens	C2
Champion Road	B3
Claremont Gardens	C4
Coniston Avenue	B1-C1
Corbets Tey Road	B1-B2-B3
Courtenay Gardens	C4
Cranborne Gardens	B3
Cranston Park Avenue	B1-C1
Derham Gardens	C2
Deyncourt Gardens	C4
Elm Avenue	B1-B2
Engayne Gardens	B4
Fairfield Avenue	C1-C2
Frimley Avenue	A4
Gaynes Court	A1-B1
Gaynes Road	B3
Gaynes Park Road	A1-B1
Grosvenor Gardens	C4
Hall Lane	B4-C4
Hedingham Road	A4
Highview Gardens	A3-B3
Hornminster Glen	A3-A4
Howard Road	B3-C3
Ingrebourne Gardens	C4
Leasway	B1-B2
Little Gaynes	B1
Little Gaynes Lane	A1-B1
Lime Avenue	A1
Maple Avenue	A1-A2
Meadow Way	B1-B2
Melstock Avenue	B1
New Place Gardens	C2-C3
Norfolk Road	A2-A3
Oak Avenue	A2-A1-B1
Park Drive	B1-C1
Roxburgh Avenue	C1-C2
Rushmere Avenue	C1-C2
St Lawrence Road	B3-C3
St Mary's Lane	A3-B3-C3
Somerset Gardens	A4
Southview Drive	A2-B2
Springfield Gardens	B2-C2
Station Road	B3
Stewarts Avenue	A2-B2
Sunnyside Gardens	B2-C2
Sycamore Avenue	A1-A2
The Grove	A1
The Shrubbery	B2-C2
Tudor Gardens	C2-C3
Upminster Road	A3
Waldegrave Gardens	B4

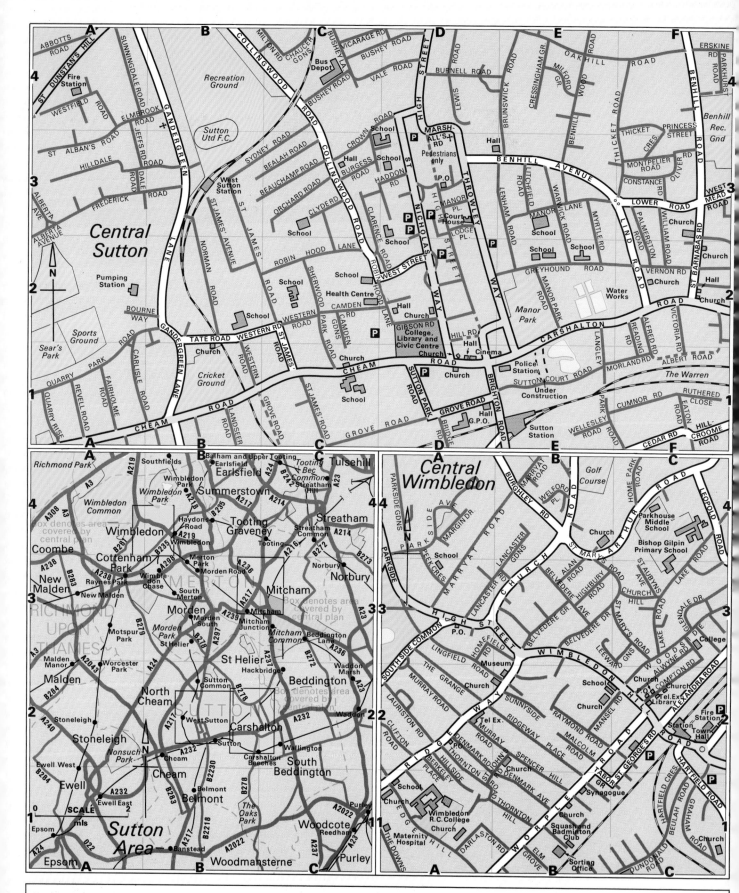

Sutton

Pleasant parks and modern shopping facilities are the chief attractions of Sutton, a residential area which was extensively developed in the 19th century. Recreation is catered for by the Westcroft Sports and Leisure Centre.

Wimbledon was a popular place for duelling in the 19th century, and it is still the site of hard fought contests — between the cream of the world's tennis players, who come here annually for the Lawn Tennis Championships, held at the end of June. The Lawn Tennis Museum can be visited in the grounds of the All England Tennis Club.

Wimbledon grew up around 16th-century Wimbledon House and has now become a pleasant residential area. The Wimbledon Theatre, in the Broadway, is popular for its Christmas pantomime, and the Polka Children's Theatre is based nearby. Wimbledon Common (scene of the duels) lies to the west and covers some 1,100 acres. An interesting restored windmill can be seen here.

Mitcham's cricket green is one of England's oldest pitches, in constant use since 1707.

Carshalton's attractive open spaces are enhanced by the River Wandle, which flows through the town and forms a pond near the centre. All Saints Church has 12th- and 13th-century features, and Little Holland, at Carshalton Beeches, has work by local craftsman Frank Dickenson.

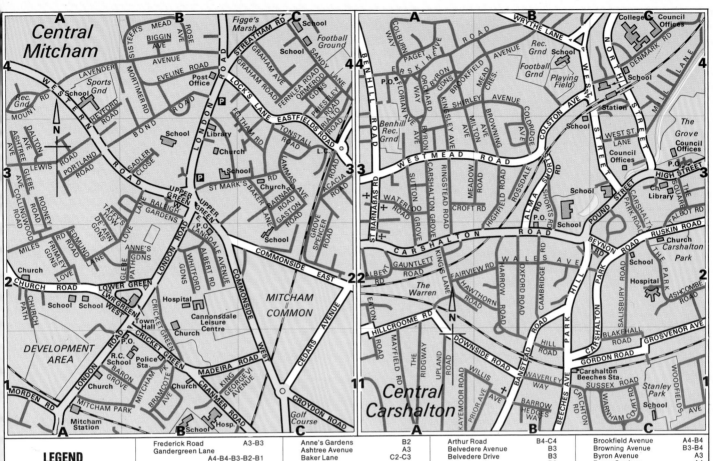

LEGEND

Town Plan

AA recommended route	
Restricted roads	
Other roads	
Buildings of interest	Hall
Car parks	P
Parks and open spaces	

Area Plan

A roads	
B roads	

Street Index with Grid Reference

Sutton

Abbots Road	A4
Albert Road	F1-F2
Alberta Avenue	A2-A3
Alfred Road	F1-F2
Bealah Road	B3-C3
Beauchamp Road	B3-C3
Benhill Avenue	D3-E3-F3
Benhill Road	F3-F4
Benhill Wood Road	E3-E4
Bourne Way	A2-B2
Bridge Road	D1
Brighton Road	D1-E1
Brunswick Road	E3-E4
Burgess Road	C3
Burnell Road	D4-E4
Bushey Lane	C4
Bushey Road	C4 D4
Camden Gardens	C1-C2
Camden Road	C2-D2
Carlisle Road	A2-A1-B1
Carshalton Road	D1-E1-E2-F2
Cedar Road	F1
Chaucer Gardens	C4
Cheam Road	A1-B1-C1-D1
Clarence Road	C3-C2-D2
Clyde Road	C3
Collingwood Road	B4-C4-C3-C2
Constance Road	F3
Cressingham Grove	E4
Crown Road	C3-C4-D4
Cumnor Road	E1-F1
Dale Road	A3
Eaton Road	F1
Elmbrook Road	A4-B4
Erskine Road	F4
Fairholme Road	A1
Frederick Road	A3-B3
Gandergreen Lane	A4-B4-B3-B2-B1
Gibson Road	D2
Greyhound Road	E2-F2
Grove Road	C1-D1
Haddon Road	C3-D3
High Street	D4-D3-D2
Hill Road	D2
Hillcroome Road	F1
Hilldale Road	A3-B3
Jeffs Road	A3-A4
Landseer Road	B1
Langley Park Road	E2-E1-F1
Lenham Road	D3-E3-E2
Lewis Road	D4
Lind Road	F2-F3
Litchfield Road	E3
Lodge Place	D3
Lower Road	F3
Manor Lane	E3
Manor Place	D3
Manor Park Road	E2
Marshall's Road	D3-D4
Milford Grove	E4
Milton Road	B4-C4
Montpelier Road	F3
Morland Road	E1-F1
Myrtle Road	E2-E3
Norman Road	B2-B3
Oakhill Road	E4-F4
Oliver Road	F3
Orchard Road	C3
Palmerston Road	F2-F3
Parkhurst Road	F4
Princess Street	F4
Quarry Rise	A1
Quarry Park Road	A1-A2
Reading Road	F1-F2
Revell Road	A1
Robin Hood Lane	B2-C2-D2
Ruthered Close	F1
St Albans Road	A3-A4
St Barnabas Road	F2-F3
St Dunstan's Hill	A4
St James' Avenue	B2-B3
St James' Road	B3-B2-C2-C1
St Nicholas Way	D1-D2-D3-D4
Sherwood Park Road	C1-C2
Sunningdale Road	A4
Sutton Court Road	E1
Sutton Park Road	D1
Sydney Road	B3-C3-C4
Tate Road	B2
Thicket Crescent	F3-F4
Thicket Road	F3-F4
Throwley Way	D4-D3-D2-E2-E1
Vale Road	C4-D4
Vernon Road	F2
Vicarage Road	C4
Victoria Road	F1-F2
Warwick Road	E2-E3
Wellesley Road	E1
West Street	D2
Western Road	B1-B2-C2
Westfield Road	A4
West Mead Road	F3
William Road	F2-F3

Mitcham

Acacia Road	C3
Albert Road	B2
Anne's Gardens	B2
Ashtree Avenue	A3
Baker Lane	C2-C3
Barnard Road	B4
Baron Grove	A1-B1
Biggin Avenue	A4
Bond Road	A3-B3-B4
Bramcote Avenue	B1
Cedars Avenue	C1-C2
Church Path	A2
Church Road	A2
Collingwood Road	A3-A2
Commonside East	B2-C2
Commonside West	B2-C2-C1
Cranmer Road	B1-C1
Cricket Green	B1-B2
Croydon Road	C1
Dalton Avenue	A3
De'Arn Gardens	A2-A3
Eastfield Road	C3-C4
Edmund Road	A2
Eveline Road	B4
Feltham Road	B4-B3-C3
Fernlea Road	C4
Frimley Gardens	A2
Galston Road	C2-C3
Glebe Avenue	A3
Glebe Path	B2
Graham Avenue	C4
Graham Road	C4
Grove Road	C2-C3
Heyford Road	A3-A4
King George VI Avenue	B1-C1
Lammas Avenue	C3
Langdale Avenue	B2
Lavender Avenue	A4-B4
Lewis Road	A3
Lock's Lane	B4-C4-C3
London Road	A1-B1-B2-B3-B4
Love Lane	A2-B2-B3
Lower Green	A2-B2
Lower Green West	A2-B2
Madeira Road	B1-C1
Miles Road	A2
Mitcham Park	A1-B1
Morden Road	A1
Mortimer Road	B4
Mount Road	A4
Ormerod Gardens	C4
Portland Road	A3
Priestley Road	C3-C4
Raleigh Gardens	B3
Rialto Road	C3-C4
Rodney Road	A2-A3
Rose Avenue	B4
St Mark's Road	B3-C3
Sadler Close	B3
Sandy Lane	C4
Sister's Mead	B4
Spencer Road	C2-C3
Streatham Road	B4-C4
Taffy's How	A3-B3
Tonstall Road	C3
Upper Green East	B3
Upper Green West	B3
Western Road	A4-A3-B3
Whitford Gardens	B2

Wimbledon

Alan Road	B3-B4
Alexandra Road	C2-C3
Alwyne Road	C2-C3

Carshalton

Arthur Road	B4-C4
Belvedere Avenue	B3
Belvedere Drive	B3
Belvedere Grove	B3
Berkeley Place	A1-A2
Beulah Road	C1
Burghley Road	A4-B4
Church Hill	C3
Church Road	A3-B3-B4
Clifton Road	A2
Compton Road	C2-C3
Darlaston Road	A1-B1
Denmark Avenue	B1
Denmark Road	A1-A2
Dundonald Road	C1
Edge Hill	A1
Elm Grove	B1
Glendale Drive	C3
Graham Road	C4
Hartfield Crescent	C1-C2
Hartfield Road	C1-C2
High Street	A3-B3
Highbury Road	B3
Hillside	A1-A2
Homefield Road	A3-B3
Home Park Road	C4
Lake Road	C3-C4
Lancaster Gardens	B3-B4
Lancaster Road	A3-B3
Lauriston Road	A2
Leeward Gardens	B3-C3
Leopold Road	C3-C4
Lingfield Road	A3-A2-B2
Malcolm Road	B2
Mansel Road	B2-C2
Margin Drive	A4
Marryat Road	A3-A4-B4
Murray Road	A2-B2
Parkside	A4-A3
Parkside Avenue	A4
Parkside Gardens	A4
Peek Crescent	A3-A4
Raymond Road	B2
Ridge Way	A1-A2-B2-B3
Ridgeway Place	A2-B2-B1
St Aubyns Avenue	C3
St George's Road	C1-C2
St John's Road	A1-B1-B2
St Mary's Road	B4-B3-C3
South Side Common	A2-A3
Spencer Hill	B1-B2
Sunnyside	B2
Tabor Grove	B1-B2
The Downs	A1
The Grange	A2-A3
Thornton Hill	A1-B1
Thornton Road	A1-A2
Welford Place	B4
Wimbledon Hill Road	B3-B2-C2
Woodside	C2
Worple Road	A1-B1-B2-C2

Carshalton

Albert Road	A2
Alma Road	B2-B3
Ashcombe Road	C2
Banstead Road	B1-B2
Barrow Hedges Way	B1
Beeches Avenue	B1
Benhill Road	A3-A4
Beynon Road	B2-C2
Blakehall Road	C1
Brookfield Avenue	A4-B4
Browning Avenue	B3-B4
Byron Avenue	A3
Byron Gardens	A4
Cambridge Road	B2
Carshalton Grove	A2-A3
Carshalton Road	A2-B2
Carshalton Park Road	B1-C1-C2-C3
Calburn Way	A4
Coldridge Avenue	B3-B4
Colston Avenue	B3-B4
Crichton Road	B1-C1
Croft Road	A3-B3
Denmark Road	C4
Downside Road	A2-A1-B1
Eaton Road	A1-A2
Erskine Road	A4-B4
Fairview Road	A2-B2
Florian Avenue	A3-A4
Gauntlett Road	A2
Gordon Road	B1-C1
Grosvenor Avenue	C1-C2
Harrow Road	B1-B2
Hawthorn Road	A2-B2
High Street	C3
Highfield Road	B2-B3
Hill Road	B1
Hillcroome Road	A1-A2
Kayemoor Road	A1
King's Lane	A2
Kingsley Avenue	A3-A4
Mayfield Road	A1
Mead Crescent	B4
Meadow Road	A3-B3
Mill Lane	C3-C4
Milton Avenue	A4-A3-B3
North Street	C3-C4
Orchard Way	A3-A4
Oxford Road	B1-B2
Paget Avenue	A4
Park Hill	B1-B2
Pound Street	B2-B3-C3
Prior Avenue	A1-B1
Ringstead Road	A2-A3
Rossdale	B3
Ruskin Road	C2-C3
St Barnabas Road	A2-A3
Salisbury Road	C1-C2
Shirley Avenue	A4-B4
Shorts Road	B2-B3
Sussex Road	B1-C1
Sutton Grove	A2-A3
Talbot Road	C2-C3
The Park	C2
The Ridgway	A1-A2
The Square	C3
Upland Road	A1
Wales Avenue	B2
Warnham Court Road	C1
Waterloo Road	A3
Waverley Road	B1
West Street	B4-C4-C3
West Street Lane	C3
Westmead Road	A3-B3
Willis Avenue	A1-B1
Woodfields Avenue	C1
Wrythe Lane	B4

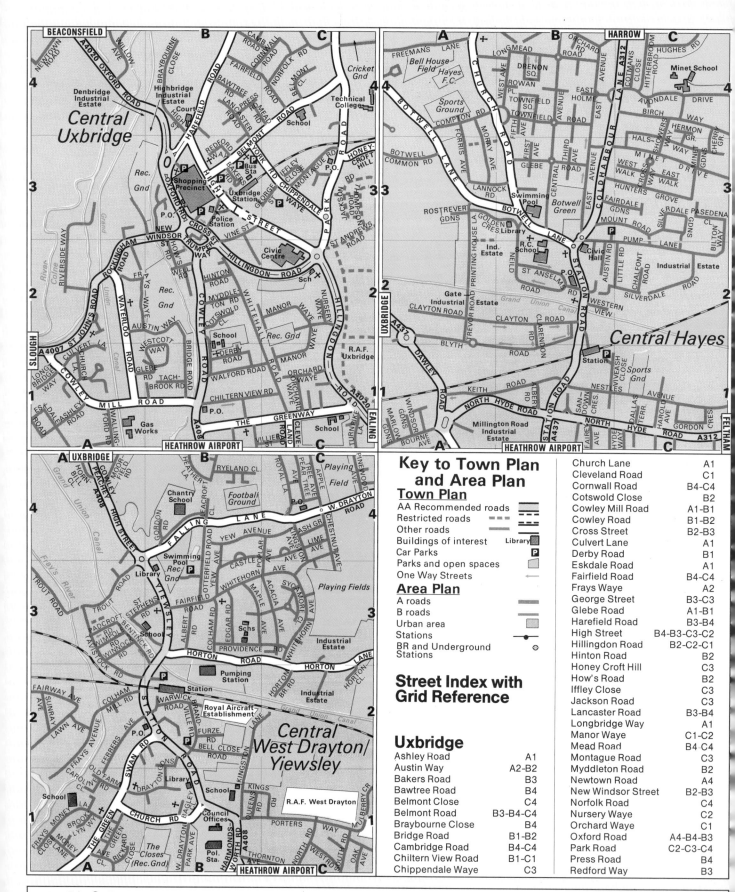

Key to Town Plan and Area Plan

Town Plan

AA Recommended roads	
Restricted roads	
Other roads	
Buildings of interest	Library
Car Parks	P
Parks and open spaces	
One Way Streets	←

Area Plan

A roads	
B roads	
Urban area	
Stations	
BR and Underground Stations	

Street Index with Grid Reference

Uxbridge

Ashley Road	A1
Austin Way	A2-B2
Bakers Road	B3
Bawtree Road	B4
Belmont Close	C4
Belmont Road	B3-B4-C4
Braybourne Close	B4
Bridge Road	B1-B2
Cambridge Road	B4-C4
Chiltern View Road	B1-C1
Chippendale Waye	C3
Church Lane	A1
Cleveland Road	C1
Cornwall Road	B4-C4
Cotswold Close	B2
Cowley Mill Road	A1-B1
Cowley Road	B1-B1
Cross Street	B2-B3
Culvert Lane	A1
Derby Road	B1
Eskdale Road	A1
Fairfield Road	B4-C4
Frays Waye	A2
George Street	B3-C3
Glebe Road	A1-B1
Harefield Road	B3-B4
High Street	B4-B3-C3-C2
Hillingdon Road	B2-C2-C1
Hinton Road	B2
Honey Croft Hill	C3
How's Road	B2
Iffley Close	C3
Jackson Road	C3
Lancaster Road	B3-B4
Longbridge Way	A1
Manor Waye	C1-C2
Mead Road	B4-C4
Montague Road	C3
Myddleton Road	B2
Newtown Road	A4
New Windsor Street	B2-B3
Norfolk Road	C4
Nursery Waye	C2
Orchard Waye	C1
Oxford Road	A4-B4-B3
Park Road	C2-C3-C4
Press Road	B4
Redford Way	B3

Uxbridge

The defence of London and south-east England was planned in an Uxbridge underground control room in World War II, and the headquarters of No 11 Corps Fighter Command was located here. RAF associations go back to 1917, when the Armament and Gunnery School of the Royal Flying Corps was established, although today the RAF Station is mainly concerned with administration.

Shortly before the arrival of the RAF, the opening of the Metropolitan and Great Western Railways had sparked off the expansion of this former market centre and staging post into a thriving suburb. It now has modern shopping precincts and sports facilities, including an artificial ski slope and a big open air swimming pool in Park Road.

Hayes has good shopping and also enjoys the leisure facilities of the modern Alfred Beck

Centre, where concerts and drama can be staged.

West Drayton is a busy suburb lying close to the M4 Motorway and Heathrow Airport. But the West Drayton Green area has been preserved and recalls the town's peaceful origins. The Grand Union Canal runs through it and is popular with boating and fishing enthusiasts.

Yiewsley was once a brick-making town, but has become a London suburb. Few buildings remain from before the 19th century.

40

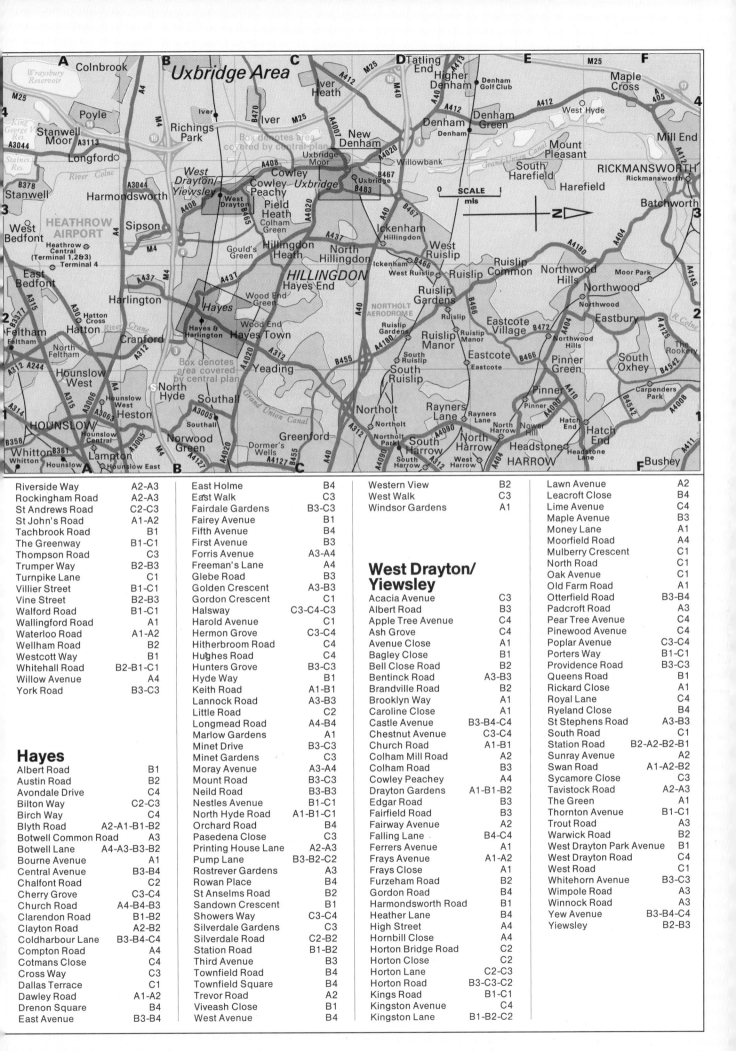

Riverside Way	A2-A3	East Holme	B4	Western View	B2
Rockingham Road	A2-A3	East Walk	C3	West Walk	C3
St Andrews Road	C2-C3	Fairdale Gardens	B3-C3	Windsor Gardens	A1
St John's Road	A1-A2	Fairey Avenue	B1		
Tachbrook Road	B1	Fifth Avenue	B4		
The Greenway	B1-C1	First Avenue	B3		
Thompson Road	C3	Forris Avenue	A3-A4		
Trumper Way	B2-B3	Freeman's Lane	A4		
Turnpike Lane	C1	Glebe Road	B3	**West Drayton/**	
Villier Street	B1-C1	Golden Crescent	A3-B3	**Yiewsley**	
Vine Street	B2-B3	Gordon Crescent	C1		
Walford Road	B1-C1	Halsway	C3-C4-C3	Acacia Avenue	C3
Wallingford Road	A1	Harold Avenue	C1	Albert Road	B3
Waterloo Road	A1-A2	Hermon Grove	C3-C4	Apple Tree Avenue	C4
Wellham Road	B2	Hitherbroom Road	C4	Ash Grove	C4
Westcott Way	B1	Hughes Road	C4	Avenue Close	A1
Whitehall Road	B2-B1-C1	Hunters Grove	B3-C3	Bagley Close	B1
Willow Avenue	A4	Hyde Way	B1	Bell Close Road	B2
York Road	B3-C3	Keith Road	A1-B1	Bentinck Road	A3-B3
		Lannock Road	A3-B3	Brandville Road	B2
		Little Road	C2	Brooklyn Way	A1
		Longmead Road	A4-B4	Caroline Close	A1
		Marlow Gardens	A1	Castle Avenue	B3-B4-C4
Hayes		Minet Drive	B3-C3	Chestnut Avenue	C3-C4
		Minet Gardens	C3	Church Road	A1-B1
Albert Road	B1	Moray Avenue	A3-A4	Colham Mill Road	A2
Austin Road	B2	Mount Road	B3-C3	Colham Road	B3
Avondale Drive	C4	Neild Road	B3-B3	Cowley Peachey	A4
Bilton Way	C2-C3	Nestles Avenue	B1-C1	Drayton Gardens	A1-B1-B2
Birch Way	C4	North Hyde Road	A1-B1-C1	Edgar Road	B3
Blyth Road	A2-A1-B1-B2	Orchard Road	B4	Fairfield Road	B3
Botwell Common Road	A3	Pasedena Close	C3	Fairway Avenue	A2
Botwell Lane	A4-A3-B3-B2	Printing House Lane	A2-A3	Falling Lane	B4-C4
Bourne Avenue	A1	Pump Lane	B3-B2-C2	Ferrers Avenue	A1
Central Avenue	B3-B4	Rostrever Gardens	A3	Frays Avenue	A1-A2
Chalfont Road	C2	Rowan Place	B4	Frays Close	A1
Cherry Grove	C3-C4	St Anselms Road	B2	Furzeham Road	B2
Church Road	A4-B4-B3	Sandown Crescent	B1	Gordon Road	B4
Clarendon Road	B1-B2	Showers Way	C3-C4	Harmondsworth Road	B1
Clayton Road	A2-B2	Silverdale Gardens	C3	Heather Lane	B4
Coldharbour Lane	B3-B4-C4	Silverdale Road	C2-B2	High Street	A4
Compton Road	A4	Station Road	B1-B2	Hornbill Close	A4
Cotmans Close	C4	Third Avenue	B3	Horton Bridge Road	C2
Cross Way	C3	Townfield Road	B4	Horton Close	C2
Dallas Terrace	C1	Townfield Square	B4	Horton Lane	C2-C3
Dawley Road	A1-A2	Trevor Road	A2	Horton Road	B3-C3-C2
Drenon Square	B4	Viveash Close	B1	Kings Road	B1-C1
East Avenue	B3-B4	West Avenue	B4	Kingston Avenue	C4
				Kingston Lane	B1-B2-C2

Lawn Avenue	A2
Leacroft Close	B4
Lime Avenue	C4
Maple Avenue	B3
Money Lane	A1
Moorfield Road	A4
Mulberry Crescent	C1
North Road	C1
Oak Avenue	C1
Old Farm Road	A1
Otterfield Road	B3-B4
Padcroft Road	A3
Pear Tree Avenue	C4
Pinewood Avenue	C4
Poplar Avenue	C3-C4
Porters Way	B1-C1
Providence Road	B3-C3
Queens Road	B1
Rickard Close	A1
Royal Lane	C4
Ryeland Close	B4
St Stephens Road	A3-B3
South Road	C1
Station Road	B2-A2-B2-B1
Sunray Avenue	A2
Swan Road	A1-A2-B2
Sycamore Close	C3
Tavistock Road	A2-A3
The Green	A1
Thornton Avenue	B1-C1
Trout Road	A3
Warwick Road	B2
West Drayton Park Avenue	B1
West Drayton Road	C4
West Road	C1
Whitehorn Avenue	B3-C3
Wimpole Road	A3
Winnock Road	A3
Yew Avenue	B3-B4-C4
Yiewsley	B2-B3

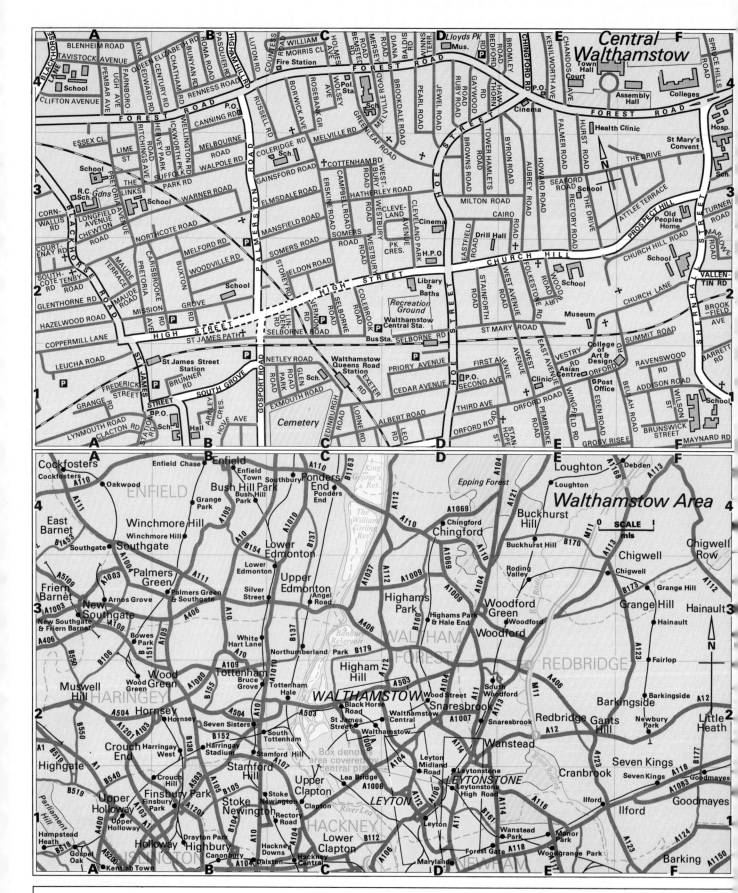

Walthamstow

Greyhound racing at Walthamstow Stadium and a seemingly endless street market — said to be the longest in Britain — are two of the top attractions of Walthamstow, an area of dramatic transformations. Covered in forest before the 15th century, it prospered as a country retreat for London's rich in the 18th and saw even greater prosperity with the industrialisation of the 19th,

culminating in the development of Britain's first internal combustion engine car, the Bremer Car, on display at Walthamstow Museum. Little of the old town has survived but Walthamstow Village has many noteworthy buildings and is now a conservation area. Among the few remaining 18th-century houses are the Clockhouse, in Wood Street, and the Water House, home of the William Morris Gallery.

Leyton was a rural retreat for wealthy London merchants, who built their mansions here in the

18th century. Few reminders of this prosperous past withstood severe wartime bombing.

Leytonstone grew up on the Roman route from Epping Forest to London, and became a 'dormitory' town with the development of the railway system. Its growth continued with extensive development and also extensive demolition, so that little of the past remains. The early 19th-century terraced houses in Browning Street are the best examples of the old town.

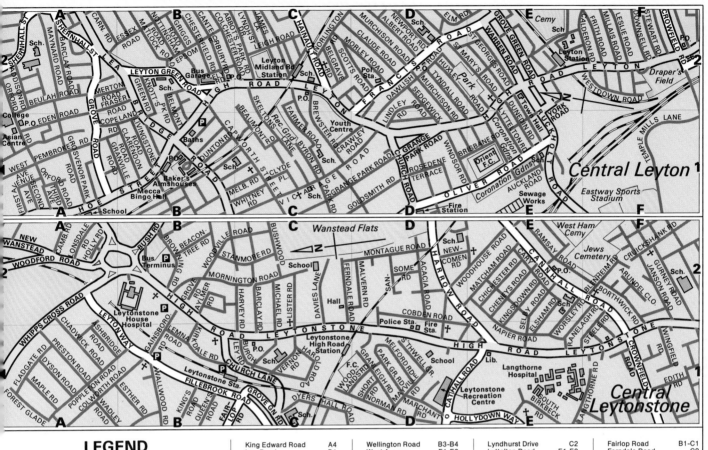

Central Leyton 1

Central Leytonstone

LEGEND

Town Plan

AA Recommended roads	
Restricted roads	
Other roads	
Car Parks	P
Buildings of interest	Station
Parks and open spaces	
Churches	†

Area Plan

A roads	
B roads	
Stations	
Borough Boundary	

STREET INDEX WITH GRID REFERENCE

WALTHAMSTOW

Addison Road	F1
Albert Road	C1-D1
Arkley Crescent	B1
Attlee Terrace	E3-F3
Aubrey Road	E2-E3-E4
Baldis Road	D4
Barrett Road	F1-F2
Bedford Road	D4
Bemsted Road	C4
Beulah Road	E1-F1
Blackhorse Lane	A4
Blackhorse Road	A2-A3
Blenheim Road	A4
Borwick Avenue	C4
Bromley Road	E4
Brookdale Road	D2-D3
Brookfield Road	E4
Browns Road	D3
Brunner Road	B1
Brunswick Street	F1
Bunyan Road	B4
Buxton Road	B2-B3
Byron Road	B4
Cairo Road	D3-E3-E2
Campbell Road	C3
Canning Road	B4
Carisbrooke Road	A2-B2
Cedar Avenue	D1
Century Road	A4-B4
Chandos Avenue	E4
Chatham Road	B4
Chewton Road	A2-A3
Chingford Road	E4
Church Hill	D2-E2
Church Hill Road	E2-F2-F3
Church Lane	E2-F2
Clacton Road	A1
Cleveland Park Avenue	D2-D3
Cleveland Park Crescent	D2-D3
Clifton Avenue	A4
Colebrook Road	C2
Coleridge Road	B3-C3-C4
Coppermill Lane	A1-A2
Cornwallis Road	A3
Cottenham Road	C3
Countess Road	C4
Diana Road	D4
East Avenue	E1-E2
Eastfield Road	D2-D3
Eden Road	E1
Edinburgh Road	C1
Eldon Road	E1
Elmsdale Road	B3-C3
Erskine Road	C2-C3
Essex Close	A3
Exeter Road	C1
Exmouth Road	B1-C1
Falmer Road	E3-E4
Farnborough Avenue	A4
Folkestone Road	E2
Forest Road	A4-B4-C4-D4-E4-F4
First Avenue	D1-E1
Frederick Street	A1
Gainsford Road	B3-C3
Gaywood Road	D4
Glen Road	C1
Glenthorne Road	A2
Gosport Road	B1-B2
Grange Road	E1
Greenleaf Road	C4-C3-D3
Grosvenor Rise East	E1-F1
Hatherley Road	D3-D3
Hawthorn Road	B2
Hazlewood Road	A2
Hervey Park Road	B3-B4
Higham Hill Road	B4
High Street	A2-B2-C2-D2
Hoe Street	D1-D2-D3-D4-E4
Holmes Avenue	C4
Hove Avenue	D1
Howard Road	E2-E3-E4
Hurst Road	E3-E4
Ickworth Park Road	B4
Jewel Road	D3-D4
Kenilworth Avenue	E4
King Edward Road	A4
Leo Road	D1
Leucha Road	A1
Linden Road	C2
Lime Street	A3
Longfield Avenue	A3
Lorne Road	C1
Luton Road	B4
Lynmouth Road	A1
Mansfield Road	B2-B3-C3
Marlowe Road	F2-F3
Maude Road	A2
Maude Terrace	A2
Maynard Road	F1
Melbourne Road	B3
Melford Road	B2
Melville Road	C3-C4
Mersey Road	C4
Milton Road	D3-E3
Mission Grove	A2-B2
Netley Road	B1-C1
Northcote Road	A2-B2-B3
Orford Road	D1-E1-F1-F2
Palmerston Road	B2-B3-B4
Park Road	C1
Pasquier Road	B4
Pearl Road	D4
Pembar Avenue	A4
Pembroke Road	E1
Pretoria Avenue	A2
Priory Avenue	D1
Prospect Hill	E2-F2-F3
Queen Elizabeth Road	A4-B4
Ravenswood Road	F1
Rectory Road	E2-E3
Renness Road	B4
Ritchings Avenue	A3-A4
Roma Road	B4
Rosebank Grove	C4
Ruby Road	D4
Russell Road	B4-C4-C3
St James Path	B2
St James Street	A1-B1
St Mary Road	D2-E2
Seaford Road	E3
Second Avenue	D1-E1
Selborne Road	B2-C2-D2
Shernhall Street	F1-F2-F3-F4
Somers Road	B2-C2-C3
Southcote Road	A2
South Grove	B1
Spruce Hills Road	F4
Stainforth Road	D2
Station Road	A1
Storey Road	C2
Suffolk Park Road	A3-B3
Summit Road	F2
Tavistock Avenue	A4
Tenby Road	D4
The Drive	E2-E3-F3
The Links	A3
Third Avenue	D1-E1
Tower Hamlets Road	D3-D4
Turner Road	F3
Valentin Road	F2
Vernon Road	D1
Vestry Road	E1-E2
Walpole Road	B3
Warner Road	A3-B3
Wellington Road	B3-B4
West Avenue	E1-E2
West Avenue Road	E2
Westbury Road	C2-C3
William Morris Close	C4
Wingfield Road	E1
Winns Terrace	D4
Wolsey Avenue	C4
Woodbury Road	E2
Woodville Road	B2

LEYTON

Abbot's Park Road	B2-C2
Addison Road	A2
Albert Road	D2
Auckland Road	E1
Barclay Road	A2
Beaumont Road	C2-C1
Belgrave Road	E2
Belmont Park Road	B1-B2
Beulah Road	A2
Brewster Road	C1-C2
Brisbane Road	D1-E1
Byron Road	C1
Calderon Road	E2-F2
Canterbury Road	B2
Carnarvon Road	A2
Capworth Street	B2-B1-C1
Chesterfield Road	B2
Church Road	D1
Clarendon Road	B1
Claude Road	C2-D2
Clyde Place	C1
Colchester Road	B2-C2
Copeland Road	A1-B1
Crowfield Road	F1-F2
Dawlish Road	D1-D2
Downsell Road	F2
Dunedin Road	E1-E2
Dunton Road	B1
Eden Road	A1-A2
Elm Road	D2-E2
Ely Road	B2
Epsom Road	B2
Essex Road	A2-B2
Farmer Road	C1-C2
First Avenue	A1
Francis Road	D1-D2-E2
Fraser Road	A2-B2
Frith Road	F2
Goldsmith Road	C1-D1
Grange Park Road	C1-D1
Granville Road	A1-B1
Griggs Road	B2
Grosvenor Park Road	A1
Grove Green Road	C2-D2
Grove Road	A1-A2
Hainault Road	C2
High Road Leyton	B1-B2-C2-C1-D1-E1-E2-F2
Hoe Street	A1-B1
Huxley Road	D2-E2-E1
James Lane	C2
Knott's Green Road	B1-B2
Lea Bridge Road	A2-B2-B1
Leigh Road	C2
Leslie Road	F2
Leyton Green Road	B2
Lindley Road	D1-D2
Livingstone Road	B1
Lyndhurst Drive	C2
Lyttelton Road	E1-E2
Matlock Road	B2
Maynard Road	A2
Melbourne Road	B1-C1
Merton Road	A2-B2
Millais Road	F2
Morley Road	C2-D2
Murchison Road	C2-D2-D1
Newport Road	D2
Norlington Road	C2
Nottingham Road	B2
Oliver Road	D1-E1
Orford Road	A1-A2
Park Road	C1
Pembroke Road	A1
Rawley Road	C1-D1
Rosedene Terrace	D1
Ruckholt Road	E2-E1-F1
Second Avenue	A1
Shernhall Street	A2
St Georges Road	E2
St Mary's Road	D2-E2
Scotts Road	C2-D2
Sedgewick Road	D1-D2
Shernall Street	A2
Skeltons Lane	C1-C2
Stewart Road	F2
Temple Mills Lane	F1
Third Avenue	A1
Tyndall Road	D1-D2
Vicarage Road	C1-D1
Warren Road	E2
West Avenue	A1
Westdown Road	E2
Windsor Road	D1-E1
Whitney Road	B1-C1
York Road	E1-E2

LEYTONSTONE

Acacia Road	D2
Arundel Close	F2
Ashbridge Road	A1
Aylmer Road	B2
Barclay Road	C1-C2
Beacontree Road	B2
Blenheim Road	F2
Borthwick Road	F1-F2
Browning Road	B2
Burghley Road	C1
Bush Road	B2
Bushwood	C2
Cambridge Road	E2
Cannhall Road	E2-F2-F1
Cary Road	E2
Cathall Road	D1-E1
Chadwick Road	A1-A2
Cheneys Road	E2
Chichester Road	E2
Church Lane	B1-C1
Cobden Road	D2-D1-E1
Colworth Road	A1-B1
Crownfield Road	F1
Cruickshank Road	F2
Davies Lane	C1
Dyers Hall Road	C1
Dyson Road	A1
Edith Road	F1
Elsham Road	E1-E2
Esther Road	A1-B1
Fairlop Road	B1-C1
Ferndale Road	C2
Fillebrook Road	B1-C1
Fladgate Road	A1
Forest Glade	A1
Gainsborough Road	B1-B2
Grove Green Road	C1
Grove Road	B2
Gurney Road	F2
Granleigh Road	D1
Harold Road	C1
Harrow Road	D2-E2-E1
Harvey Road	C1-C2
High Road Leytonstone	B2-B1-C1-D1-E1-F1-F2
Holly Road	A2
Hollydown Way	D1-E1
Janson Road	F2
King's Road	B1
Kingsdown Road	E1-E2
Kirkdale Road	B1
Langthorne Road	E1-F1
Lemna Road	B1
Leyton Way	A2-A1-B1
Lister Road	C1-C2
Lonsdale Road	A2
Malvern Road	D2
Maple Road	A1
Marchant Road	D1
Matcham Road	D2-E2
Mayville Road	D1
Melford Road	D1
Michael Road	C1-C2
Montague Road	C2-D2
Mornington Road	B2-C2
Napier Road	E1-E2
Newcomen Road	D2
New Wanstead	A2
Norman Road	C1-D1
Poppleton Road	A1-B1
Preston Road	A1
Queen's Road	B1
Ramsay Road	E2-F2
Ranelagh Road	E1-E2-F2
Sansome Road	D2
Selby Road	E1-E2
Short Road	C1-D1
South Birkbeck Road	E1
Southwell Grove	D1
Stanmore Road	B2-C2
Steele Road	E1-F1-F2
Vernon Road	C1
Wadley Road	A1
Wallwood Road	B1
Whipps Cross Road	A1-A2
Wingfield Road	F1
Woodlands Road	C1-D1
Woodford Road	A2
Woodhouse Road	D2-E2
Woodville Road	B2-C2
Worsley Road	E1-E2

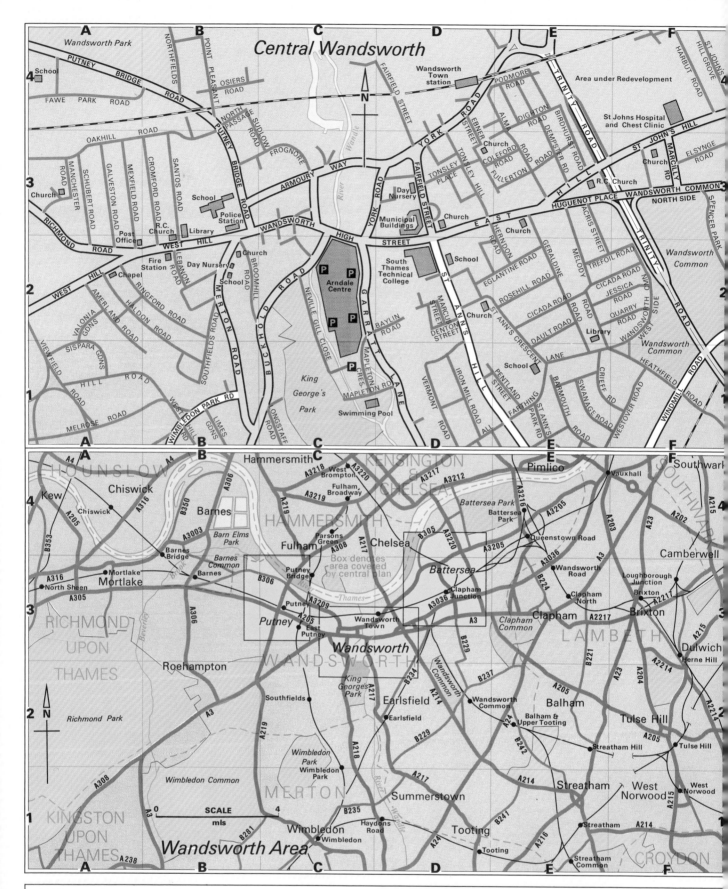

Wandsworth

Oscar Wilde and Great Train Robber Ronald Biggs both spent time in Wandsworth, as inmates of the prison which is one of its best-known features. This is an industrialised area which grew when the railways arrived in the 19th century.

Battersea boasts two great landmarks for Londoners: its park and its power station. Battersea Park was opened in 1853 under royal command, and has since undergone a number of improvements and innovations, including the Festival of Britain Gardens, designed by Sir Osbert Lanchester and John Piper, and established in 1951. The power station dominates the London skyline with its four distinctive chimneys. Designed by Sir Giles Scot and first used in 1937, it is no longer operating but may become the centrepiece of a proposed leisure park. Battersea's Old Town Hall has been converted into an Arts Centre and many theatrical and musical productions are staged there.

Putney gives an overall impression of being distinctly Victorian and Edwardian. It grew into a fashionable London suburb during the 18th century, and continued to undergo a good deal of development right up until the 1920s, but since then has seen relatively little change. Putney Bridge has been the starting point for the University Boat Race since 1845.

44

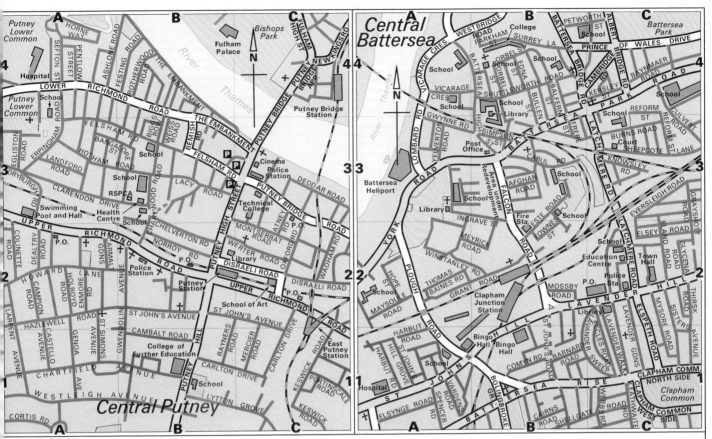

Street Index with with grid reference

Wandsworth

Acris Street	E2-E3
All Farthing Lane	D1-E1
Alma Road	D4-E4-E3
Amerland Road	A2-A1-B1
Armoury Way	B3-C3-D3
Barmouth Road	E1
Baylin Road	C2-D2
Birdhurst Road	E3-E4
Broomhill Road	B2
Buckhold Road	B1-C1-C2-C3
Cicada Road	E2-F2
Coleford Road	D3-E3
Crieff Road	E1-F1
Cromford Road	B2-B3
Dault Road	E1-E2
Dempster Road	E3-E4
Dighton Road	D3-E3-E4
East Hill	D2-D3-E3
Ebner Street	D3-D4
Eglantine Road	D2-E2
Elsynge Road	F3
Fairfield Street	C4-D4-D3
Fawe Park Road	A4-B4
Frognore	B3-C3
Fullerton Road	D3-E3
Galveston Road	A2-A3
Garratt Lane	C2-C1-D1
Geraldine Road	E1-E2-E3
Haldon Road	A2-B2-B1
Harbut Road	F4
Heathfield Road	E1-F1
Herndon Road	D3-E3-E2
Hill Road	A1-B1
Huguenot Place	E3-F3
Iron Mill Road	D1
Jessica Road	E2-F2
Lebanon Road	B2
Limes Gardens	C1
Longstaff Road	A3
Manchester Road	C1-C2
Mapleton Crescent	C1-D1
Mapleton Road	F3
Marcilly Road	E1-E2-E3
Melody Road	A1-B1
Melrose Road	B1-B2
Merton Road	A2-A3
Mexfield Road	C1-C2
Neville Gill Close	B4
Northfields	B4
North Passage	A3-B3
Oakhill Road	B4-C4
Osiers Road	D1-E1
Pentland Street	D4-E4
Podmore Road	D4
Point Pleasant	B4
Putney Bridge Road	A4-B4-B3
Quarry Road	E2-F2
Richmond Road	A2-A3
Ringford Road	A2-B2
Rosehill Road	E2
St Ann's Crescent	D2-E2-E1
St Ann's Hill	D2-D1-E1
St Ann's Park Road	E1
St John's Hill	E3-F3-F4
St John's Hill Grove	F4
Santos Road	B2-B3
Schubert Road	A2-A3-A1
Sispara Gardens	A1
Southfields Road	B1-B2
Spencer Park	F2-F3
Sudlow Road	B4-B3-C3
Swanage Road	E1-F1
Tonsley Hill	D3
Tonsley Place	D3
Trefoil Road	E2-F2
Trinity Road	E4-E3-F3-F2-F1
Valonia Gardens	A2
Vermont Road	D1
Viewfield Road	A1-A2
Wandsworth Common North Side	F3
Wandsworth Common West Side	F1-F2
Wandsworth High Street	B2-B3-B4
West Hill	A2-B2-B3
West Hill Road	A1
Westover Road	E1-F1
Wimbledon Park Road	B1
Windmill Road	F1-F2
York Road	C3-D3-D4-E4

Putney

Ashlone Road	A4-B4
Atney Road	C2-C3
Bangalore Street	A3-B3
Bemish Road	B3
Biggs Row	B3-B4
Cambalt Road	B1
Campion Road	A2
Carlton Drive	B1-C1-C2
Carmalt Gardens	A2
Castello Avenue	A1-A2
Charlwood Road	B2-B3
Chartfield Avenue	A1-B1
Chelverton Road	B2-B3
Clarendon Drive	A3-B3
Colinette Road	A2-A3
Cortis Road	A1
Dealtry Road	A2
Deddar Road	C3
Disraeli Road	B2-C2
Dryburgh Road	A3
Egliston Road	A3
Enmore Road	A2
Erpingham Road	A3-A4
Felsham Road	A3-B3-C3
Festing Road	B4
Fulham High Street	C4
Genoa Avenue	A1-A2
Gwendolin Road	B1-B2
Hazlewell Road	A2-B2
Holroyd Road	A2
Horne Way	A4
Hotham Road	A2-B2
Howard Lane	A2-B2
Keswick Road	C1
Lacy Road	B3
Landford Road	A3
Larpent Avenue	A1-A2
Lower Richmond Road	A4-B4-B3
Lytton Grove	B1-C1
Mercier Road	C1-C2
Montserratt Road	B3-C3-C2
New Kings Road	C4
Norroy Road	B2
Oxford Road	C2
Pentlow Street	A4
Portinscale Road	C1
Putney Bridge	C3-C4
Putney Bridge Approach	C4
Putney Bridge Road	C2-C3
Putney High Street	B2-B3-B3
Putney Hill	B1-B2
Rayners Road	B1-B2
Rotherwood Road	B4
St John's Avenue	B2-C2-C1
St Simons Avenue	A1-A2
Sefton Street	A4
The Embankment	B4-B3-C3
Upper Richmond Road	A3-A2-B2-C2-C1
Wadham Road	C2
Weiss Road	B3
Werter Road	B2-C2
Westleigh Avenue	A1-B1

Battersea

Afghan Road	B3
Albert Bridge Road	C4
Balfern Street	B3-B4
Barnard Road	B1
Battersea Bridge Road	B4-C4
Battersea High Street	A4-B4-B3
Battersea Park Road	B3-B4-C4
Battersea Rise	A1-B1-C1
Baynmaer Road	C4
Bolingbroke Grove	B1
Bullen Street	B3-B4
Burns Road	C3
Cabul Road	B3
Cairns Road	B1
Cambridge Road	B4-C4
Clapham Common North Side	C1
Clapham Common West Side	C1
Comyn Road	B1
Culvert Road	C3-C4
Eccles Road	C1-C2
Edna Street	B4
Eland Road	C2-C3
Elsey Road	C2
Elspeth Road	C1-C2
Elsynge Road	A1
Este Road	B2-B3
Eversleigh Road	C2-C3
Falcon Road	B2-B3
Fownes Street	B2
Frere Street	B3
Glycena Road	C2
Grant Road	A2-B2
Grayshott Road	C2-C3
Gwynne Road	A3-B3
Harbut Road	A1
Hope Street	A2
Ingrave Street	A3-B3-B2
Kersley Street	C4
Knowsley Road	C3
Latchmere Road	C2-C3-C4
Lavender Gardens	C1-C2
Lavender Hill	B2-C2
Lavender Sweep	C1-B1-B2-C2
Lavender Walk	C1-C2
Leathwaite Road	C1
Lombard Road	A3-A4
Maysoule Road	A2
Meyrick Road	A2-B2
Mossby Road	B2
Mysore Road	C1-C2
Orbel Street	B4
Parkham Street	B4
Petworth Street	B4-C4
Plough Road	A1-A2
Prince of Wales Drive	B4-C4
Reform Street	C3-C4
St John's Hill	A1-B1-B2
St John's Hill Grove	A1
St John's Road	B1-B2
Sheepcote Lane	C3
Shellgate Road	B1-C1
Shuttleworth Road	B4
Simpson Street	B3
Sisters Avenue	C1-C2
Spencer Road	A1
Surrey Lane	B4
Thirsk Road	C1-C2
Thomas Baines Road	A2
Vardens Road	A1
Vicarage Crescent	A4-B4
Webbs Road	C1
Westbridge Road	A4-B4
Winstanley Road	A2-B2
Yelverton Road	A3
York Road	A2-B2-B3

LEGEND

Town Plan

- AA Recommended roads
- Other roads
- Restricted roads
- Buildings of interest — Cinema
- Churches
- Car Parks — P
- Parks and open spaces

Area Plan

- A roads
- B roads
- Stations — Mitcham
- Borough Boundary

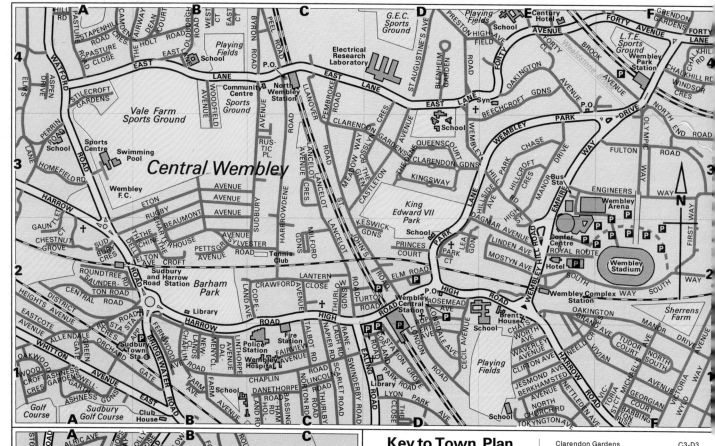

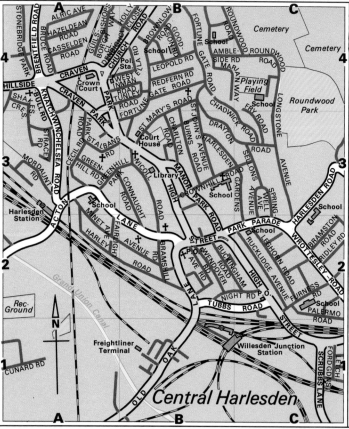

Key to Town Plan and Area Plan

Town Plan

AA Recommended roads	
Other roads	
Restricted roads	
Buildings of interest	Library
Churches	†
Car Parks	P
Parks and open spaces	
BR and Underground Stations	⊖

Area Plan

A roads	
B roads	

Street Index with Grid Reference

Central Wembley

Allendale Road	A1-A2
Ashness Gardens	A1
Aspen Drive	A4
Babbington Rise	F1
Bassingham Road	C1
Beaumont Avenue	B2-B3-C3
Beechcroft Gardens	D3-E3-E4
Berkhamstead Avenue	E1
Bleheim Gardens	D4
Bridgewater Road	B2-B1
Brook Avenue	E4-F4
Byron Road	C4
Camden Crescent	A4
Castleton Avenue	C3-D3-D4
Cecil Avenue	D1-D2
Central Road	A2-B2
Chalkhill Road	F4
Chaplin Road	B1-C1
Charter House Avenue	B3-B2-C2
Chatsworth Avenue	E2-E1
Chestnut Grove	A2

Clarendon Gardens	C3-D3
Clifton Avenue	E1
Copeland Avenue	C2
Copeland Road	D1
Crawford Avenue	C2
Dagma Avenue	D2-E2
Dalmeny Close	B1
Danethorpe Road	C1
Dean Court	B4
District Road	A2-B2
Ealing Road	C1-D1
Eastcote Avenue	A2-A1
East Court	B4
East Lane	A4-B4-C4-D4-E4
Elm Road	D2
Elms Lane	A4-A3
Elton Avenue	B2
Empire Way Drive	E2-E3-F3-F4
Engineers Way	E3-F3
Eton Avenue	A2-A3-B3-C3
Fairview Avenue	C1
Farm Avenue	B1
Fernwood Avenue	B1
First Way	F2-F3
Forty Avenue	E4-F4
Forty Close	E4
Forty Lane	F4
Gauntlet Court	A3-A2
Georgian Court	F1
Grand Avenue	E2-E1-F1
Greengate	A1
Grendon Gardens	F4
Harrowdene Road	C2-C3-C4
Harrow Road	A3-A2-B2-C2, E2-E1-F1
Heights Avenue	A2-A1
Highfield Avenue	D4-E4
High Road	C2-D2-E2
High Street	E3
Hillcroft Crescent	E3
Hill Road	A4
Hillside Avenue	E3
Holland Road	C1
Holt Road	A4-B4
Homefield Road	A3
Jesmond Avenue	E1
Keswick Gardens	C2-D2
Kingsway	D3
Lancelot Avenue	C3
Lancelot Crescent	C3
Lancelot Road	C2
Lantern Close	C2
Lea Garden	D2
Lincoln Road	C1
Linden Avenue	E2

Wembley

Scene of FA and Rugby League Cup Finals, the 1948 Olympic Games, the 1966 World Cup Finals, countless concerts, public appearances and events such as the open air Mass during the 1982 Papal visit, Wembley Stadium is the chief claim to fame for this residential and industrial area.

Originally designed as a centrepiece for the British Empire Exhibition of 1924, the stadium complex includes Wembley Arena, used for horse shows and ice spectaculars, a national squash centre and a modern hotel. Nearby stands the Wembley Conference Centre, opened in 1976, which also provides facilities for exhibitions and concerts. Wembley itself began as a rural district centred around Wembley Park, but saw extensive development after the opening of the London to Birmingham railway in the mid-19th century.

Harlesden Animal shows, handicrafts, music and drama take over Roundwood Park in the north every year, for the annual Brent show. A village until the late 19th century, Harlesden grew when railway yards and sidings were established here and several major industrial companies arrived.

Willesden is another area which has undergone a good deal of housing and industrial development since the mid-19th century, when Willesden Junction was built. Places of interest include St Mary's Church, which is of Norman origin.

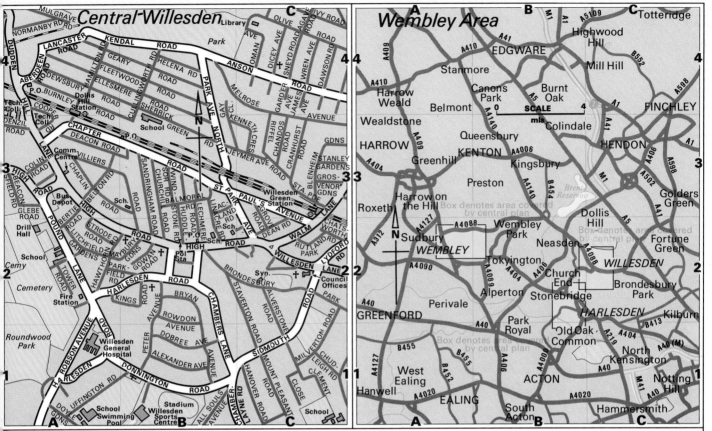

Central Willesden / Wembley Area

Linthorpe Avenue	B1	Victoria Avenue	F1-F2
Llandover Road	C4-C3	Victoria Court	F1
London Road	D2-D1	Vivian Avenue	E2-E1-F1
Lonsdale Avenue	D1-D2	Watford Road	A4-A3-A2
Lyon Park Avenue	D1	Waverley Avenue	E1
Monor Drive	E3	Wellgarth	A1
Meadow Way	C3	Wembley Hill Road	D4-D3-E3-E2
Milford Gardens	C2	Wembley Park	E3-E4
Mostyn Avenue	E2	West Court	B4
Napier Road	C2-C1	Whitton Avenue East	A1-B1
Neeld Crescent	E1-E2-F2	Windsor Crescent	F4
Nettleden Avenue	E1	Woodcroft	A1
Newlands Close	B1	Woodfield Avenue	B4-B3
North Church Road	E1	Wyld Way	F1
North End Road	F4-F3		
North South	F1		
Norton Road	C1	**Willesden**	
Oakington Avenue	E4		
Oakington Manor Drive	E2-F2-F1	Aberdeen Road	A4
Oakwood Crescent	A1	Acland Road	B3
Oldborough Road	B4	Agave Road	C4
Olympic Way	F4-F3	Alexandra Avenue	B1
Orchard Gate	A1-B1	All Souls Avenue	E3
Park Chase	E3	Alverstone Road	C1-C2
Park Court	D2	Anson Road	B4-C4
Park Lane	D2-D3-E3	Beaconsfield Road	A3
Park Road	D1	Belton Road	A3
Pasture Close	A4	Bertie Road	A2-A3
Pasture Road	A4	Bleneheim Gardens	C3
Peel Road	C4	Brondesbury Park	B2-C2
Pembroke Road	C3-C4	Bryan Avenue	B1-B2
Perrin Road	A3	Burnley Road	A4-A3-B3
Petts Grove Avenue	B2	Chamberlayne Road	C1-D1
Preston Road	D4	Chambers Lane	B1-B2
Princes Court	D2	Chandos Road	C3
Queenscourt	D3	Chaplin Road	A3-B3
Ranelagh Road	C1	Chapter Road	A3-B3
Rosemead Avenue	D2	Chatsworth Road	C2
Rossyln Crescent	D3-D4	Churchill Road	B2-B3
Rountree Road	A2	Clement Close	C1
Royal Route	E2	Colin Road	C3
Rugby Avenue	A2-B2-B3-C3	Cooper Road	A3-A4
Rupert Avenue	D1-D2	Cranhurst Road	C3
Rustic Place	C3	Cullingworth Road	B3-B4
St Augustines Avenue	D4	Dawson Road	C4
St John's Road	C3-C2-D2	Dean Road	C2
St Michael's Avenue	F1	Denzil Road	A3
Saunderton Road	A2-B2	Dewsbury Road	A4-B4
Scarle Road	C1	Dicey Avenue	C4
South Way	E2-F2	Dobree Avenue	B1
Stapenhill Road	A4	Donnington Road	A1-B1
Station Approach	B2-B1-A1	Doyle Gardens	A1
Station Crescent	A2-A1	Dudden Hill Lane	A3-A4
Station Grove	D1-D2	Ellesmere Road	A4-B4
Stilecroft Gardens	A4	Fleetwood Road	A4-B4
Sudbury Avenue	C2-C3-C4	Gardener Avenue	C4
Sudbury Crescent	A2	Gary Close	B3-B4
Swinderby Road	C1	Geary Road	A4-B4
Sylvester Road	B2-C2	Glebe Road	A3
Talbot Road	C1	Gowan Road	B2
The Chine	B2	Grosvenor Gardens	C3
The Close	D1	Grove Road	C2-C3
The Croft	B2	Hamilton Road	A4
The Dell	B2-A2	Hanover Road	C1
The Dene	D3	Harlesden Road	A1-A2-B2
The Fairway	B4-A4-B4	Hawthorn Road	A2-B2
The Glen	C3	Helena Road	B4
Thurlby Road	C1	High Road	A3-A2-B2-C2
Thurlow Gardens	C2	Huddlestone Road	B2-B3
Tokyngton Avenue	E1	Ivy Road	C4
Tudor Court	F1	James Avenue	C4
Turton Road	C2-D2		

Jeymer Avenue	B3-C3	Fry Road	C3-C4
Kendal Road	A4-B4	Furness Road	C2
Kenneth Crescent	B3-C3	Goodson Road	B4
Kings Road	A2-B2	Greenhill Park	A3-B3
Lancaster Road	A4	Greenhill Road	A3
Lechmere Road	B2-B3	Guilsborough Close	A4
Linacre Road	B2-B3	Harlesden Gardens	B3-C3-C2
Litchfield Gardens	A2	Harlesden Road	C2-C3
Lydford Road	C2	Harley Road	A3-A2-B2
Maybury Gardens	A2-B2	Hazeldean Road	A4
Melrose Avenue	B4-C4-C3	High Street	B3-B2-C2-C1
Milverton Road	C1-C2	Hillside	A4
Mount Pleasant Road	C1	Holly Close	B4
Mulgrave Road	A4	Knatchbull Road	A3-A4
Normandy Road	A4	Leghorn Road	C2
North Park Avenue	B3-C3-C2	Leopold Road	B4
Olive Road	C4	Letchford Gardens	C1
Oman Avenue	C4	Longstone Avenue	C3-C4
Park Avenue	B3-B4	Manor Park Road	B2-B3
Parkfield Road	A2-B2	Marian Way	B4
Peter Avenue	B1-B2	Minet Avenue	A2-A2-B2
Pound Lane	A2-A3	Mordaunt Road	A3
Riffel Road	C3-C4	Nicoll Road	B2-B3
Robson Avenue	A1-A2	Night Road	B2-C2
Rowdon Avenue	B1-B2	Old Park Lane	A1-B1-B2
Rutland Park	C2	Palermo Road	C2
St Paul's Avenue	B3-C3-C2	Park Parade	B2-C2
Sandringham Road	B2-B3	Park Road	A3
Sherrick Green Road	B3-B4	Redfern Road	B4
Sidmouth Road	B1-C1-C2	Ridley Road	C2
Sneyd Road	C4	Roundwood Road	B4-C4
Stanley Gardens	C3	Rucklidge Avenue	C2
Station Parade	C3	St Albans Road	A3
Staverton Road	C1-C2-B2	St Mary's Rod	B3-B4
Strode Road	A2-A3	St Johns Avenue	B3-B4
Tower Road	A2	Scrubbs Lane	C1
Uffington Road	A1-B1	Sellons Avenue	C2-C3
Villiers Road	B2-B3-A3	Shakespeare Crescent	A3-A4
Walm Lane	C2-C3	Springwell Avenue	C2-C3
Willesden Lane	C2	Stonebridge Park	A4
Windsor Road	B3	Stracey Road	A3
Wren Avenue	C4	Tubbs Road	B2-C2
		Tunley Rod	A4-B4
		Wendover Road	B2
Harlesden		West Ella Road	A4-B4
		West Inman Road	A4-B4
Acton Lane	A2-A3-A2-B2	Winchelsea Road	A3
Alric Avenue	A4	Wrottesley Road	C2
Ambleside Road	B4-C4		
Avenue Road	B2		
Bishops Way	A4		
Bramston Road	C2		
Branshill Road	B2		
Brentfield Road	A4		
Brownlow Road	B4		
Bruce Road	A4		
Buckingham Road	B2-C2		
Burns Road	B3-B4		
Casselden Road	A4		
Cecil Road	A3		
Chadwick Road	B4-C4-C3		
Charlton Road	B3		
Church Road	A4-B4		
Connaught Road	A3-B3-B2		
Craven Park	A3-A4		
Crownhill Road	B3-C3		
Cunard Road	A1		
Denbigh Close	A4		
Drayton Road	B4-B3-C3		
Fairlight Avenue	A2		
Fortune Gate	B3-B4		

Heathrow Airport

Biggest and busiest airport in the United Kingdom, handling more international traffic than any other airport in the world, Heathrow broke its own records on 31 August 1980, when 112,880 passengers passed through. 1983 saw a total of 26,749,200 travellers, assisted by the 45,000-strong staff of the British Airports Authority and the 74 airline companies from 68 countries which operate scheduled services from the airport. Aircraft go to over 90 countries, and Heathrow's No 1 runway, 2.42 miles (3.9km) in length, is the longest used by civilian aircraft in the United Kingdom.

It all began when the site was transferred from the Air Ministry to the Ministry of Civil Aviation on 1 January 1946. On 31 May 1946, it opened as London (Heathrow) Airport, superseding the Airport of London at Croydon, established in 1928. This resulted in the operation of direct services between the United Kingdom and the United States of America. On 16 December 1955, the first three permanent buildings were opened by the Queen, and all three passenger terminals are now interlinked by pedestrian subways with moving walkways. The terminals are situated in the central area of the airport, and are also linked to the M4. A fourth terminal is under construction on the south-eastern side of the airport.

Terminal 1 is used by United Kingdom and Irish airlines for domestic and European flights, and for British Airways flights to and from certain destinations in North America. Terminal 2 is used by other European airlines except for the Irish airlines. Terminal 3 is the one used by intercontinental airlines going to Africa, America, Asia and Australia.

In 1966, the newly appointed British Airways Authority took over the responsibility for both Heathrow and the second airport at Gatwick (the two are linked by a frequent daily helicopter service). Direct rail access came in 1977 when the Underground's Piccadilly Line was extended and in the same year, Heathrow Central Station opened.

Today the Queens Building Roof Gardens and viewing gallery allow visitors to admire the aircraft and to watch the airport at work. There is a small admission charge for this.

Visitors who have come to the Queens Building Roof Gardens can also take refreshments there, at one of the many restaurants to be found throughout the airport. All three passenger terminals have licensed restaurants where full meals are served, and there are also grill bars providing hot meals. Light refreshments can also be bought.

Multi-storey car parks are sited at each of the passenger terminals for short term car parking. Heathrow also has long term car parks, situated on the northern perimeter road. A free coach carries passengers between the long term car parks and the terminals. During the night (from midnight to 6am), passengers wanting this service can contact the coach base on the special direct line telephones which are in use at the pick-up points.

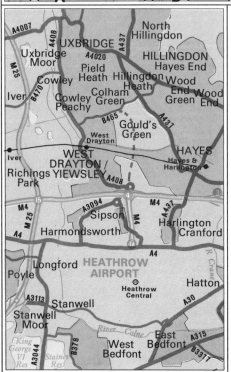